HEINEMANN HI

EXPANSION, TRADE AND INDUSTRY

STUDY UNITS

HEINEMANN
EDUCATIONAL

John Child

Heinemann Library,
an imprint of Heinemann Publishers (Oxford) Ltd,
Halley Court, Jordan Hill, Oxford OX2 8EJ

OXFORD LONDON EDINBURGH MADRID
ATHENS BOLOGNA PARIS MELBOURNE
SYDNEY AUCKLAND SINGAPORE TOKYO
IBADAN NAIROBI HARARE GABORONE
PORTSMOUTH NH (USA)

First published 1993

93 94 95 96 97 98 10 9 8 7 6 5 4 3 2 1

**British Library Cataloguing in Publication Data is available
from the British Library on request.**

ISBN 0–431–07338–4

Designed by Ron Kamen, Green Door Design Ltd, Basingstoke

Illustrated by Barry Atkinson and Jeff Edwards

Printed in China

The front cover shows a Yorkshire miner standing in front of a
Blenkinsop locomotive. An engraving by R. & D. Havell, 1813.
Reproduced by permission of the British Museum.

Acknowledgements

The author and publisher would like to thank the following for
permission to reproduce photographs:

Agricultural Economics Unit, Oxford: 2.2F
Bodleian Library, Oxford: 1.1D, 5.2B
Bridgeman Art Library: 1.1H, 2.6A, 2.8B, 2.10B, 2.12B, 3.1B,
3.2B, 3.4C, 4.5C, 6.1A
British Library: 1.1F
British Museum: 5.1B
Celtic Picture Library: 2.4C
Christie's: 1.1E
Corcoran Gallery of Art, Washington DC: 3.3A
ET Archive: 4.3C, 5.1C
Mary Evans Picture Library: 2.1E, 2.11B, 2.12D, 3.2E, 4.2D,
4.3D, 4.4E, 4.4F, 4.6C
Guildhall Library/Bridgeman Art Library: 1.1B, 2.8C, 2.11A
Hulton Deutsch Collection Ltd: 5.3E

Illustrated London News: 3.4B
Institute of Agricultural History and Museum of English Rural
Life: 2.2H, 2.3C
London Transport Museum: 6.1B
Mansell Collection: 1.1G, 2.5A, 2.5C, 2.5D, 2.7C, 2.9C,
4.2C, 4.6B, 5.1D, 5.3E
Metropolitan Museum of Art, New York: 2.6D
Museum of London: 2.9B
National Maritime Museum, San Francisco: 2.12A
National Museum of Wales: 2.4A
National Museums and Galleries on Merseyside: 2.2G, 2.7A
National Portrait Gallery: 1.1A
Natural History Museum, London: 4.5F
Out of the West Publishing/Linda Mackie Collection: 2.3B
Picturepoint: 3.2D, 4.2E
Quadrant Picture Library: 2.12F
Ann Ronan Picture Library: 4.2C
Royal Holloway College/Bridgeman Art Library: 2.11C
Science Museum, London: 2.4D
Statens Museum for Kunst, Copenhagen: 4.1G
Tate Gallery, London: 4.5G
TUC: 5.3C
Victoria & Albert Museum: 3.2C
Weidenfeld & Nicolson: 5.2E

Every effort has been made to contact the copyright holders of
material reproduced in this book. Any omissions will be
rectified in subsequent printings if notice is given to the
publisher.

We would also like to thank HarperCollins Publishers Ltd for
permission to use Source A on page 10, which was taken from
Agriculture 1730-1872 by J. R. S Whiting, originally published
by Evans Brothers, 1971.

Details of Written Sources
In some sources the wording or sentence structure has been
simplified to ensure that the source is accessible.

R. J. Cootes, *Britain Since 1700*, Longman, 1968: 5.2C
R. Floud, *History Today* (vol. 33), May 1983, pages 36-40: 4.3B
C. P. Hill, *A Survey of British History*, Arnold, 1968: 5.2D
Simon Mason, *Transport and Communication 1750-1980*,
Blackwell, 1985: 2.12C
Peter Mathias, *The First Industrial Nation*, Methuen, 1969:
2.1C
Trevor May, *An Economic and Social History of Great Britain
1760-1970*, Longman, 1987: 2.12F
D. Richards and J. W. Hunt, *Modern Britain 1783-1964*,
Longman, 1950: 3.2A
E. P. Thompson, *The Making of the English Working Class*,
Penguin, 1963: 4.3A
R. J. Unstead, *Freedom and Revolution*, Macdonald, 1972: 2.1A
Cecil Woodham-Smith, *The Reason Why*, Heinemann
Educational, 1971: 3.4A

CONTENTS

1.1 Britain in 1750

In 1750, Britain was made up of England, Scotland and Wales. George II was king. When he died in 1760, he was followed by his grandson, George III. The king and his ministers governed with the help of Parliament. The landed classes dominated Parliament. We can follow their debates in personal diaries and in 'Hansard', a daily record of debates in Parliament, which began at about this time. Ordinary people had little to do with the government of their country. In some places they could vote for MPs in elections. But there was no secret vote. Election records show that people usually voted the way their landlord or employer told them.

Britain often quarrelled with other countries in Europe. The Catholic countries of Europe, such as France, Austria and Spain regarded Britain as an enemy. Britain had a much smaller army than these countries. But she had a powerful navy and a growing number of **colonies**. Records of imports and exports at this time show that British merchants were trading further and further afield. Britain was in competition with France, Spain and Holland to gain colonies and trade.

A SOURCE

George III in his coronation robes. He was king for 60 years. He was a major figure in the events covered by the first half of this book.

B SOURCE

A cartoon by Gillray showing an election speech. What impression of the elections does this cartoon give you? Some of the crowd are very excited and are waving their hats. The woman on the left is probably the reason; she is handing out free gin, paid for by one of the candidates.

C

SOURCE

A scene outside a public house showing the game of shuffle-board.

Most people in Britain lived in the countryside. Much of the land was owned by the Church or the heads of great aristocratic families, like the Dukes of Norfolk or Marlborough. Their family records give details of huge estates scattered all over the country. Only slightly less wealthy were the gentry. These were squires who owned large estates, but usually all in one county. Sir Robert Walpole, who had been prime minister until 1742, was from this class. The gentry farmed some of their land and rented out the rest to tenant farmers. Farmers employed labourers to help them on the land. Most people in the countryside worked in farming or jobs linked to farming like blacksmiths.

The aristocracy had large country houses, like Blenheim Palace in Oxfordshire or Longleat in Wiltshire. You can still visit their fabulous dining rooms, libraries and bedrooms. Many of their landscaped gardens, lakes and mazes also survive. The country pastimes of the wealthy were hunting and fishing outdoors, and music, dice and billiards indoors. Poorer people went to the public houses for their entertainment, where they drank ale and played skittles and bowls. At holiday times they went to fairs with cockfights and boxing or cricket matches. It is harder for historians to find personal accounts of the lives of the poor.

D

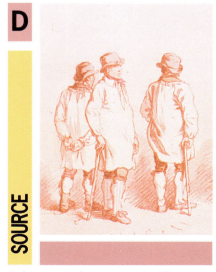

SOURCE

Labourers in the countryside. The smocks they are wearing were typical all over the country.

London was the biggest town in Britain, with a population of about half a million. There are many paintings of London at this time. Bristol, Liverpool and Hull were important ports. Leeds, Norwich and Bath were also large towns.

The wealthy enjoyed life in the towns. There were assembly rooms for dancing and music and clubs for gambling. People could stroll in pleasure gardens such as Vauxhall and Ranelagh in London. The less wealthy went to coffee shops and bath-houses. James Boswell's biography of Dr Samuel Johnson gives us a rich picture of this lifestyle. But most people in the towns were very poor. They lived in crowded, draughty houses. Poor people spent time in the dram houses, which sold cheap gin. Drunkenness was a serious problem.

This was also an age of great works of art. Jonathan Swift wrote 'Gulliver's Travels' and Daniel Defoe wrote 'Robinson Crusoe'; Dr Johnson wrote the first general dictionary of the English language. David Garrick was the greatest actor of the age and George Frederick Handel came to England and became a famous musician. There were many great artists, such as George Stubbs and Thomas Gainsborough. The books and paintings of the day give us a vivid picture of the time. So do the cartoons and engravings of Gillray, Rowlandson and Hogarth.

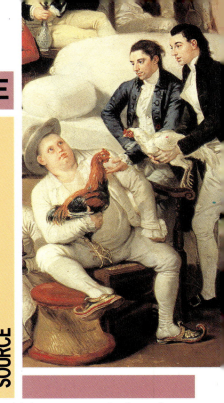

E SOURCE

Cockfights were a popular form of entertainment. Detail from a painting by John Zoffany (c. 1790).

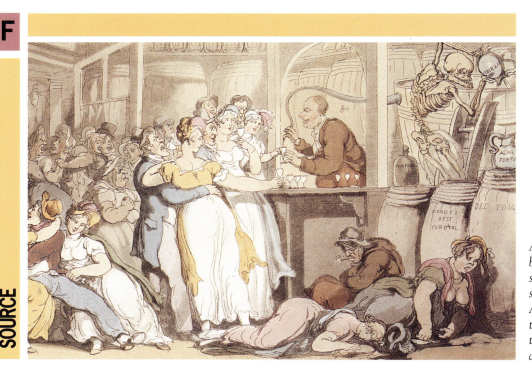

F SOURCE

A tinted engraving by Rowlandson, showing a dram shop. In 1751 an Act was passed to tax spirits. After this, drunkenness declined.

G

SOURCE

The Ranelagh pleasure gardens in London. Some guests are in fancy dress; some are dancing round a maypole. The house on the left is in the Queen Anne style; the other buildings show the fashion for classical arches and pillars.

H

SOURCE

A watercolour by Rowlandson, dated 1787. Poor diet and dental care left many people without teeth. Transplanting artificial or human teeth was one remedy. Hospitals and battlefields were the main sources of human teeth.

George III

George III (1738–1820) became king in 1760, at 22 years of age, when George II died of a heart attack while sitting on the lavatory. George II was not clever, but he was hard working, religious and dignified. He was a powerful political figure; no minister could survive without his support. In 1788, George III became ill. He probably had **porphyria**, a blood disease which poisons the brain. It has symptoms similar to madness. George III recovered in 1789, but the illness kept recurring. He drifted out of political life and died, grey haired and insane, when he was 81 years old.

2.1 Population

In 1750 the population of Britain was about 7 million and rising slowly. The first national census, in 1801, showed that the population had reached 10.5 million. By 1851, the figure was 21 million; by 1901, 37 million. The rise was greatest in industrial towns like Birmingham, Manchester and Glasgow, but even rural counties grew. The rise was most obvious in the midlands and north of England, South Wales and the lowlands of Scotland. Historians are not sure whether more **births** or fewer **deaths** caused the rise. Births and deaths were not recorded until 1836. Before that, the only records were baptism and burial registers kept by the Church.

A SOURCE

Church records show that the increase was due to a slightly rising birth rate and a much reduced death rate. People lived longer because there were better living conditions and more food; cheap gin was put out of reach by taxes. But the most important cause was babies surviving infancy, mothers surviving childbirth and people recovering from illness because of better medical care.

From 'Freedom and Revolution' by R. J. Unstead, 1972.

C SOURCE

The parish registers became very inaccurate after 1780. The records of burials underestimate deaths by as much as 25%. There were more births than the records of baptisms show. Historians have shown that medical changes could not have improved death rates much. Advances were patchy and costly. Living conditions in the towns got worse, not better, until about 1840. More births, caused by earlier marriage and better job prospects caused the rise.

From 'The First Industrial Nation' by Peter Mathias, 1969.

B SOURCE

A graph showing the number of baptisms and burials from 1740–1900. These figures are taken from parish registers, records kept by busy clergymen, at a time when fewer people were going to church. Some historians don't trust these figures.

D SOURCE

Why has the population of Birmingham increased from 23,000 in 1750 to 30,000 in 1770? It must be because of an increase in employment. People are getting married earlier (and having more children) because the children they have do not cause them great expense. Any child, as soon as it can use its hands, can provide the family with money.

From 'Political Arithmetic' by Arthur Young, 1774.

The Cow Pock 1802. A cartoon by Gillray. In 1796, Edward Jenner showed that patients
vaccinated with the harmless disease of cattle called 'cowpox' became immune to the deadly smallpox.
Many people were very suspicious of the idea, as this cartoon shows.

The population rose rapidly until about 1880. Large families were common. After that the death rate began to fall because of better living conditions and medical care. But the birth rate fell even faster. Parents had fewer children. The size of families began to fall to the size we are used to today. The population increase slowed down.

The rise in population changed Britain. It led to overcrowding and poor **living conditions** in most cities. These cities grew rapidly; by 1900 most British people lived in **cities**. The increased population also caused changes in the British economy. More people meant more **demand** for food and other goods. Farmers and manufacturers made big **profits**. More people also meant more **workers**, so farmers and manufacturers could find plenty of labour without having to pay high **wages**. The following units describe these changes in the economy.

Malthus

The Reverend Thomas Malthus (1766–1834) was an influential writer. In 1798 he wrote *An Essay on Population*, in which he claimed the population of Britain was rising dangerously fast. The census result of 1801 seemed to prove him right.

Malthus said food supplies would fall behind the growing population, there would not be enough jobs; poverty and starvation would follow. This was already happening in Ireland. Malthus's book caused concern and influenced political ideas. Many politicians said that it was wrong for the government to help the poor and hungry. This would allow them to have more children, making the problem worse. But Malthus was wrong. New methods of farming produced much more food; factories produced more jobs. The Industrial Revolution saved Britain from mass starvation.

2.2 The Agricultural Revolution

The traditional method of farming was called the **open field system**. It was very wasteful. The cultivated land around a village was normally divided into three great fields. Every farmer had small **strips** of land in each of the fields. Every year, all the farmers had to grow the same crops; **wheat** (for bread) in one field and **barley** (for ale) in another. Each farmer's strips were widely scattered, so it was difficult to move equipment between strips. Weeds spread from strip to strip easily, despite the **baulks** or unused pathways between them. The third field was left **fallow** (nothing grown) so that the soil could recover. Another underused area was the **common land**. This was left as a place for the villagers to gather free firewood, fruit and berries and graze their animals. This was cheap, but it made it impossible to control the breeding of the animals.

Once the **population** began to rise, there were more and more people needing food. Farmers could charge **higher prices**, make **bigger profits** and still sell all their produce. This made them keen to produce as much food as possible. To increase their produce, they changed their **methods of farming**. Landowners needed more control over their own land before they could introduce more efficient methods of farming. They started to swap strips to consolidate their land into larger units. Sometimes landowners would meet up and agree to divide the land into separate farms. This was called **enclosure**. If they could not all agree, the larger landowners could get Parliament to pass an **Enclosure Act** to force the redistribution of the land. Soon these Acts began to include the enclosure of the common land. Between 1750 and 1810, there were over 4,000 Enclosure Acts.

Once the land was enclosed, farmers could introduce new methods. Some farmers, like **Viscount Townshend**, adopted the Norfolk four course **rotation of crops**. This involved using one field for wheat, one for clover, one for barley or oats and one for turnips or swedes. These crops were swapped around the fields every year. No fields had to be kept fallow because the clover and the swedes naturally replaced the nutrients which the

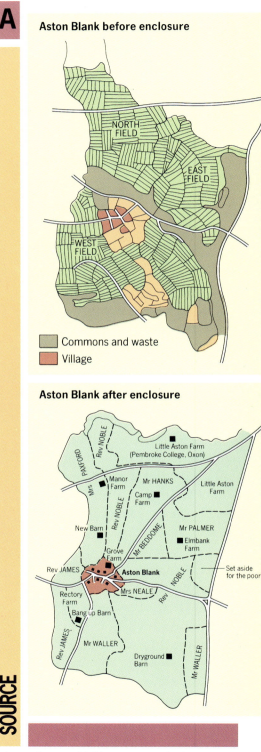

Aston Blank before enclosure

NORTH FIELD

EAST FIELD

WEST FIELD

Commons and waste

Village

Aston Blank after enclosure

Rev NOBLE
PAXFORD
Mrs
Rev NOBLE
Little Aston Farm (Pembroke College, Oxon)
Manor Farm
Mr HANKS
Camp Farm
Little Aston Farm
New Barn
Rev NOBLE
Mr BEDDOME
Mr PALMER
Elmbank Farm
Grove Farm
Rev JAMES
Aston Blank
Mrs NEALE
Rev NOBLE
Set aside for the poor
Rectory Farm
Bang up Barn
Rev JAMES
Mr WALLER
Dryground Barn
Mr WALLER

SOURCE

The enclosure of fields at Aston Blank, Gloucestershire, in 1752.

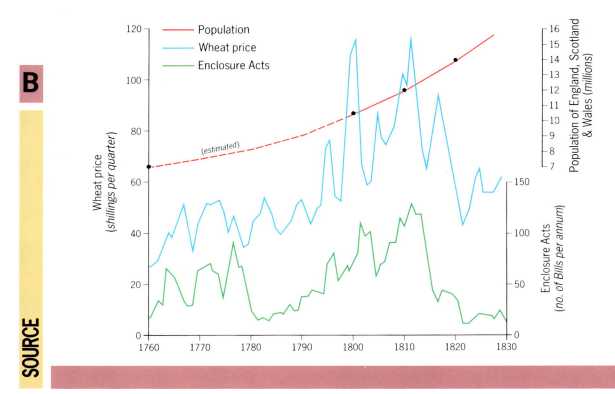

This graph shows the link between growing population, rising prices and enclosures.

wheat and barley or oats used up. The fields of clover and swedes could be used to graze animals, whose manure enriched the soil as they fattened on the crops. This produced higher yields of grain and meat.

Other farmers experimented with new machinery. **Jethro Tull** invented a **seed drill** which could be pulled along behind a horse. The drill spread the seeds evenly, in rows and then covered them up as protection against the birds. Tull later invented a **horse-drawn hoe** which could be dragged through the fields weeding between the lines of crops.

Some farmers used **selective breeding**. This involved using selected animals to develop new breeds: cattle which produced more milk and meat, sheep which gave more meat and wool. **Robert Bakewell** developed the New Leicester sheep. The **Colling brothers** bred the Durham shorthorn cattle. These animals could then be sold to farmers to breed with their own livestock, to produce improved animals.

These changes in farming had far reaching effects. The **quantity of food** produced increased. The **quality of food** also improved. This helped the population grow. But farms couldn't employ all of the extra people in the countryside; many had to move to the **towns** to find work. This was good for industry. It gave employers plenty of cheap **labour**.

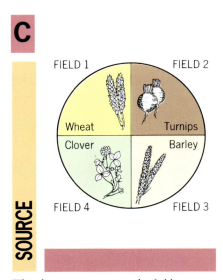

This diagram represents the fields on a farm using the four course rotation. Can you draw a diagram to show what would happen in the following year?

Not everyone benefited from the enclosures, though. Many **yeomen farmers**, who owned their own small farms, could not afford the cost. Some had to sell up and become labourers. Villagers suffered from the loss of the **common land**: the ground they sometimes got in exchange was no real compensation.

This first phase of the **agricultural revolution** came to a peak in the years between 1790 and 1810. For most of this time Britain was at war with France. Imports of cheap food from the continent were cut off. This made prices rise even faster and farmers made record profits from enclosures and new farming methods. When the war ended in 1815, cheap imports returned. For a while there was more food in Britain than its 10 million people could buy and prices fell. Farmers' profits fell and there was a period of depression in agriculture. This lasted until about 1840. By then, the population had risen to about 18 million. Prices rose again and farmers began to look for even more efficient methods to make the most of the possible profits. They started a second phase of the agricultural revolution called **high farming**.

High farming was the application of science and technology to agriculture. Many farmers began to use new machinery, new fertilizers and better drainage methods.

Machinery was introduced to save labour. For example, seed drills and threshers were used widely for the first time. From about 1850, steam power began to be used to drive farm machinery. Steam-powered reapers and threshers could do the work of many men.

E **Wheat output in England and Wales**

1750	15m quarters
1790	19m quarters
1820	25m quarters

Notice that the biggest increase came after 1790. A quarter was one-fourth of a hundredweight of wheat (about 12.5 kilograms).

F In 1710, the cattle and sheep sold at Smithfield Market weighed on average as follows:
cattle   370lb
sheep   28lb

Now they weigh:
cattle   800lb
sheep   80lb

Sir John Sinclair, President of the Board of Agriculture, 1795.

D

Cotswold sheep (1866), exaggerated in size by the artist.

G

A Lincolnshire bull painted by George Stubbs in 1790.

An 8 horse-power steam threshing machine in 1860. The machine was used to separate the seed-corn from the straw.

Better **drainage** methods stopped seed and crops rotting in the ground and so increased yields. Steam engines could pump excess water from the black silts of the fens for just 2s 6d (12p) per year. Factories could produce clay pipes for drainage trenches at a cost of less than £1 per thousand and Fowler's mole plough could lay them for less than £5 per acre.

Fertilizers were also used to increase yields. Guano (bird droppings rich in phosphates) was imported at a rate of over 100,000 tons a year from Peru in the 1850s; other natural fertilizers included crushed bones and soot. Superphosphates, nitrates and other artificial fertilizers were imported from Germany or bought from factories at home. In 1842 Sir John Lawes opened a chemical fertilizer factory in London.

As a result of these developments, farm production rose by 70% between 1840 and 1870, although the amount of farmland stayed the same. The number of farmworkers dropped by 300,000. This second phase of the agricultural revolution, from 1840 to 1870, was the **golden age** of farming. Unfortunately it didn't last long.

Townshend

Viscount Townshend (1674–1738) was a British diplomat to Europe. While in Europe, he learned about the use of clover and turnips as part of **crop rotations**. In 1730, he argued with the prime minister, Sir Robert Walpole, and retired from politics. He returned to his estates in Norfolk determined to make his farms more efficient. He made the farmers who rented his land use crop rotations which gave plenty of turnips and other winter fodder. He was nicknamed *Turnip Townshend* as a joke, but, in fact, his well publicized success made his methods popular with other rich landowners.

2.3 Agricultural Depression

The 1870s was a decade of **bad weather** in Britain. Crops went mouldy in the ground; machinery was bogged down in the muddy fields. Three million sheep died of foot rot in 1879 alone.

Normally, poor output would have sent prices up and this would have cushioned the blow for farmers. But by the 1870s they had a second problem – **foreign competition**. **Steam ships** on the oceans and **railways** in foreign continents had opened up vast new areas of food production. Huge quantities of cheap grain came flooding in from the prairies of North America. Cheap wool was shipped in from Australia and New Zealand. These imports kept prices low and British farmers' profits fell badly. Hundreds of British grain and sheep farmers went bankrupt. **Refrigeration** was invented at this time, too. This enabled shiploads of frozen beef and other goods to come from New Zealand, Australia and Argentina.

A **SOURCE**

August was very unfavourable. Pastures on clay land were as wet as in the middle of winter. Grass was all trodden away and cattle sank in to their knees. The quality of both wheat and barley was wretched. No corn to sell and nobody cared to buy British produce. Vast quantities of grain pouring in from the USA. In this year, the first shipment of refrigerated beef arrived in Britain.

From the official Agricultural Records for 1879.

B **SOURCE**

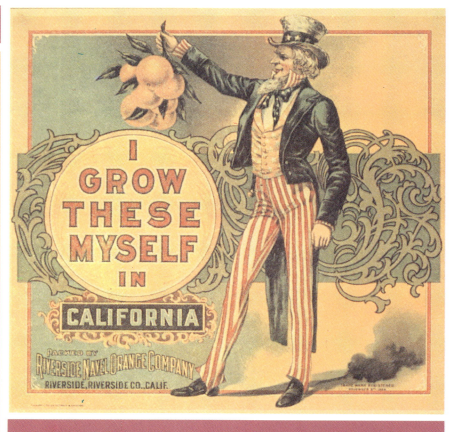

An orange box label dated about 1898.

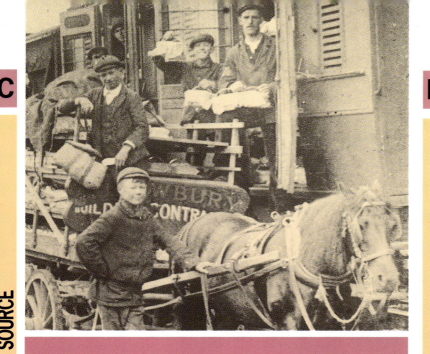

C

SOURCE

British farm labourers loading fresh strawberries onto a train bound for London in 1906.

Farmers had to adapt. Those who could switched from grain to vegetables, fruit, flowers or dairy produce. These did not suffer so badly from foreign competition. The railways were a help. For the first time, farmers could get fresh flowers, eggs, butter and fruit to the large towns quickly. Even farmers producing meat had some hope. They could buy the cheap imported grain to feed to their livestock. If they could get their beef, lamb and chicken to market fresh, they had an advantage over the imported frozen or canned meat. Some farmers were therefore able to survive. Even so, about 300,000 farm labourers had lost their jobs by 1900. Britain now produced only one third of her food and the century ended less happily for farmers than it had begun.

Arch

Joseph Arch (1826–1919) founded the National Agricultural Labourers' Union in 1872. This was a difficult time for farm labourers. Farmers were using more machines to do farm work. They were keeping more cattle and sheep, which needed fewer workers than arable farms. This caused unemployment and low wages. Joseph Arch was a Methodist preacher; a forceful speaker who urged farm workers to press for better working conditions and higher wages. For a time, the union had 100,000 members. Arch also campaigned for the vote for workers and he became MP for Norfolk in 1888.

D

1867
5m cattle in Britain

1914
7m cattle in Britain

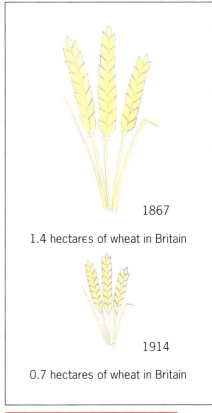

1867
1.4 hectares of wheat in Britain

1914
0.7 hectares of wheat in Britain

SOURCE

Changes in agricultural output.

2.4 Power

Horses were still by far the most common form of power used in Britain in 1750. They were used to pull, lift and carry things too heavy for men. Coalmines used horses to power the winding gear which lifted the coal out of the shafts (see Source A). Wind and water were also used to generate power. Waterwheels and windmills turned the millstones that ground corn into flour, for example. But there were problems with these sorts of power. Horses had limited strength and energy. Wind and water were not reliable (see Source B). Water power required fast-flowing streams, which only existed in some parts of the country.

A SOURCE

A painting by Paul Sandby of a coalmine in about 1786. A horse powered gin is being used to lift the coal.

B SOURCE

May 29. Another very warm day, and the dry weather is much against us as the river Ribble is very low; in the afternoons our looms go very slow for want of water. August 28. There were 30 mills stopped in Blackburn this month for want of water, and will not start again until wet weather sets in.

An extract from a Lancashire weaver's diary.

C SOURCE

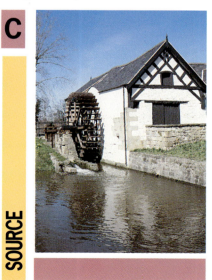

The watermill at Rossett, Clwyd.

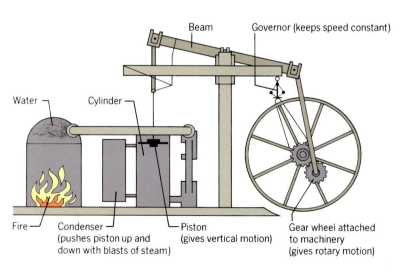

A diagram to explain the Boulton and Watt steam engine, pictured on the opposite page.

Watt

James Watt (1736–1819) has been called the inventor of the steam engine. Generations of pupils were told that he got the idea while watching a kettle boil.

Nothing could be further from the truth. Savery and Newcomen had designed steam engines before Watt. He worked for years to make a precision machine which used less coal and could create rotary as well as vertical motion.

Steam was another source of power. In 1698, **Dr Thomas Savery** had invented a steam engine to pump out the water that flooded tin mines in Cornwall. In 1712, **Thomas Newcomen** made an improved version. There were about 300 of these engines in use by 1800. But they used lots of coal and only produced vertical motion, driving something up and down. They could not be used to power machines needing rotary motion, where things were driven round and round.

These problems were solved by **James Watt**. In 1763, he decided that he could improve Newcomen's engine. As he had no money to test his improvements, he was helped by Dr John Roebuck, the owner of the Carron Ironworks in Scotland. But in 1773, Roebuck went bankrupt. Watt's invention seemed lost. Then **Matthew Boulton**, a factory owner from Birmingham, who had heard of Watt's ideas, offered to become his partner. Watt went to work, using the engineering skills of William Murdoch, Boulton's foreman, to help him put his ideas into practice. At one stage, they couldn't make a good enough cylinder for the steam-driven piston. They were rescued by the skill of John Wilkinson, a well-known ironmaster, who made one for them. Eventually, Watt and Boulton produced a new steam engine. It was much better than Newcomen's and it could drive rotary motion (see Source D). Steam engines could now be used for all kinds of work. They made cheap mass production possible. They were at the heart of the changes in industry we call the **Industrial Revolution**. The next few units explain these changes.

D SOURCE

A steam engine designed in 1788 by James Watt.

2.5 Textiles ✓

In 1750, woollen cloth was Britain's most important product. The **woollen industry** was spread as widely as East Anglia, the south west of England, Yorkshire and Scotland. The raw wool was first spun into yarn on a spinning wheel; then this yarn was woven into cloth on a loom. Workers usually did the spinning and weaving in their own cottages. This was called the **domestic system**. Families shared the work; spinning was done by women; weaving by men. But the growing population created more demand for clothes. This promised profits for anyone who could produce large amounts of cheap cloth.

Spinning wool before the industrial revolution.

In 1733, **John Kay** had invented the **flying shuttle**. It was a device added to the hand-loom to speed up weaving. This was followed in 1765, by the **spinning jenny**, invented by **James Hargreaves**. This machine could spin six threads of yarn at once. Both of these machines could be used in the workers' cottages. By 1788, there were 20,000 spinning jennies in use and the woollen industry was booming.

More change was to come. In 1769, **Richard Arkwright** patented the **water frame**. This machine for spinning yarn was powered by a water wheel. In 1779, **Samuel Crompton** made an even better machine called the **mule**.

It was many years before an efficient weaving machine was made. Then **Edmund Cartwright** invented a **power loom** in 1785. It was not widely used until it was improved, first by William Horrocks in 1803 and then by Richard Roberts in 1812.

These machines changed the woollen industry. They were too large for workers' cottages. They needed a water wheel or a steam engine to power them. The new machines were housed in **mills** or **factories**. Women and children could look after the machines; there was less work for men. Mills became concentrated in areas of the country close to fast-flowing streams or, even better, near sources of cheap coal for the steam engines. Another change was that these machines could

At Hyde are two factories, sited between a torrent which supplies the engines with water and two coalmines which supply fuel. Mr Ashton employs 1500 workpeople of both sexes. One immense room, filled with looms, contains 400 of them. The houses lived in by the workers form long and large streets. Mr Ashton has built three hundred houses which he lets at 3s (15p) per week.

An extract from a report written in about 1840.

C

SOURCE

Cotton spinning during the industrial revolution.

produce cotton cloth. Cotton was more comfortable to wear; it soon became more popular than woollen cloth. The cotton industry was mainly based in Lancashire. By 1830, 80% of cotton spinning was steam powered and there were 100,000 steam-powered looms for spinning.

The changes in **textiles** are typical of the Industrial Revolution. They made cotton a vital part of the economy in Britain. By 1850, about 350,000 people worked in the cotton industry. About 200,000 were women and 15,000 children. Another 200,000 worked in woollens. Cotton provided 35% of British exports and remained the biggest export product until the Second World War.

Arkwright

Richard Arkwright (1732–92) began his working life as an apprentice barber. He ended up owning factories worth about £800,000. His success came from his 'water frame'. By the 1760s, new inventions meant that cotton weavers could work much faster than spinners.

Arkwright improved a spinning machine invented by Lewis Paul in the 1730s. It was driven by water power and soun strong cotton yarn extremely fast, on long rows of spindles. He built factories full of water frames in Lancashire and Derbyshire. They earned him wealth, fame and a knighthood.

D

SOURCE

The Cloth Hall, Leeds in 1813. Wealthy merchants at work. Yorkshire became the centre of the woollen industry. First its fast flowing Pennine streams and later the nearby coalfields provided cheap power for the mills. Hull became the chief port for its exports.

2.6 Iron and Steel

In 1750 Britain's iron industry was still very small. It was sited mainly in Shropshire, near sources of iron ore and supplies of timber which provided the charcoal used as fuel in the furnaces. Several inventions brought major changes in the iron industry.

Charcoal was becoming scarce and expensive. In 1709, **Abraham Darby** began using **coke** instead of charcoal to make **pig iron** at his ironworks at **Coalbrookdale** in Shropshire. Slowly others copied his methods. This meant that ironworks were not tied to woodland. Areas which had iron ore and coal deposits could now start making cheap **cast iron**.

However, this cast iron was very brittle and had few uses. By 1784, **Henry Cort** was using a new method for turning the cast iron into **wrought iron**. He reheated the cast iron in a **forge**, then 'puddled' or stirred it to remove most of the impurities. After it cooled, he passed the metal through grooved rollers which removed the rest of the impurities. This **puddling and rolling** made it possible to produce wrought iron cheaply.

In 1828, **Robert Neilson** made ironmaking even cheaper by reducing the amount of fuel needed. He did this by making the bellows pump hot air into the furnaces, not cold. This improvement was only used in Scotland for a while and it gave the iron industry there a boost. (See Source B.) In 1840, **James Naysmith** produced a steam-powered hammer which made forging much quicker and easier. It replaced the light trip hammers used before.

The ironmasters were keen to show how useful iron could be. Abraham Darby's grandson (Abraham Darby III), built a famous iron bridge across the River Severn. John 'iron-mad' Wilkinson was even buried in a metal coffin. It was now possible to build the tools, machines, bridges, and railways of the Industrial Revolution. (See Source C.) Ironmaking became one of Britain's most important industries. British iron production in 1750 was about 30,000 tons; by 1830, it was 1 million tons; by 1870, 6 million tons.

Steel remained very expensive to make until after 1850. Britain's total output was still only 60,000 tons.

Making iron and steel in 1750
Iron ore was dug from the ground. It was melted in a furnace with charcoal made to glow red hot by blasts of air from bellows. When the molten ore cooled it became **pig iron** or **cast iron**, an impure, brittle metal, used for pots, pans and pipes.

The impurities were removed by heating the cast iron and hammering it in the forge. This made **wrought iron**, a tough but pliable metal used for nails, chains, etc.

Steel is a very hard and flexible metal made from pig iron with carbon and manganese added.

A

SOURCE

A painting from 1772 by Joseph Wright showing a forge. The red hot pig iron is being held on an anvil under a trip hammer. These were driven by water wheels and later by steam engines.

But in 1856, **Henry Bessemer** invented a **'converter'** which blasted oxygen through molten pig iron to remove impurities. Then carefully-measured carbon and manganese could be added to make steel. Bessemer set up a steel works in Sheffield in 1858. In 1867, **William Siemens** invented a new way of making steel, the **open hearth** method. But neither method worked well with British iron ore, which contained too much phosphorus. Britain relied on imported ore. By 1880, British steel production reached 2 million tons. But German and American steelmaking grew faster.

B
SOURCE

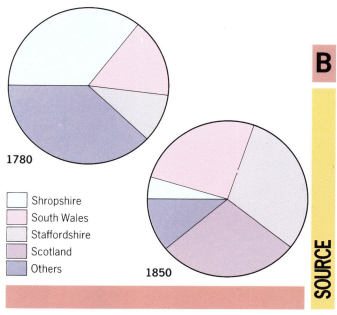

1780

	Shropshire
	South Wales
	Staffordshire
	Scotland
	Others

1850

The location of British iron production.

Wilkinson

John Wilkinson (1728–1808) was an ironmaster. In 1774, he invented a lathe for boring the barrels of cannons and made a fortune during the Seven Years War (1756–63). He later used the same machine to make cylinders for James Watt's steam engines. He had a gift for applying ideas. He was one of the first to use coke smelting; he used a steam engine to power his trip hammers. He was a great salesman for iron goods. He became known as 'iron mad Wilkinson'. He helped Abraham Darby build the first iron bridge in 1779 and built a cast iron chapel for his Methodist friends. He built the first ever iron barge in 1787 and, in the next year, sent 40 miles of iron pipes for Paris's water supply. When he died, he was buried in an iron coffin.

C
SOURCE

Since cast iron has got all the rage,
And scarcely a thing's made
    without it,
As I live in this cast iron age,
I mean to say something about it.
We have cast iron fenders and
    grates,
We have cast iron pokers and
    tongs sir,
And soon we'll have cast iron
    plates,
And cast iron small clothes ere
    long sir.

Extracts from a popular ballad from the 1820s.

D
SOURCE

'Forging the Shaft', a painting dated 1877. The steam hammers had not taken all of the heavy work out of the forging process.

21

2.7 Coal

In 1750, coalmining was a small, but important industry. It was centred in the north east of England and produced about **5 million tons** per year, mainly to heat people's homes. After 1750 the demand for coal increased. There were more homes to heat, and steam engines and the iron industry used coal for fuel. Later, railways used coal too. This growing demand promised big profits. Landowners were willing to invest their money to mine deeper and deeper in search of coal. But deeper mining meant more technical problems.

Water caused **flooding** in the mines. Pumps driven by the **steam engines** of Newcomen, Savery and Watt were the solution here. By 1775, there were 400 steam driven pumps on coalfields. But **ventilation** was a more difficult problem. Gases seeped out of the coal deposits. Some suffocated the miners; others exploded on contact with the flames which were the miners' only source of light. To remove these gases, deep mines were given two shafts. A **furnace** at the bottom of one heated the air. As the hot air rose it pulled fresh air down the other shaft. This fresh air was circulated underground by opening and closing **trap doors**. In 1815, Sir Humphrey Davy invented a **safety lamp**. A flame burned in the lamp behind a wire gauze which prevented contact with the explosive gas. Later, **steam-powered fans** were used to blow fresh air into the mines, but these were not common until after 1860.

The down-cast shaft is called the John Pit. It is 204 yards deep and has a steam engine for drawing the coal and a horse gin for lifting the men when the machine is crippled. The air furnace shaft is called the William Pitt. It has only a horse gin. Trap doors, attended by boys about 8 years old, are placed to divert the air through proper channels. The air is accelerated through the workings by a large fire in this up-cast shaft.

A description of the Felling Colliery in Durham.

The pithead of a coalmine. Horses and mules are still being used for transport. But there is a steam-powered water pump in the centre of the painting and steam-powered winding gear on the left.

Lifting and carrying the coal was the third major problem. **Horses** were kept underground and used for pulling coal wagons along the shafts. Workers – often women – were used to carry the coal in baskets up ladders to the surface. **Horse gins** were used as lifting gear at the pithead. However, steam power brought improvements. From 1800 steam engines were used to wind cages carrying the miners or the coal up the shafts. **Wire ropes**, invented in 1834 and made from wrought iron, made this much safer. **Steam-powered wagon ways** carried coal around the pithead at some mines from about 1810; later, **trains** carried coal cheaply to all parts of Britain.

By 1900, 'King Coal' was a major industry, spread over many parts of Britain. It produced nearly **200 million tons** per year and employed over one million people. About a quarter of the coal produced was exported. The rest provided fuel for industry and heat for the growing population.

The coalfields of Britain in about 1800.

- Central Scotland
- North East
- Yorkshire, Derbyshire, Notts.
- South Wales
- Midlands

C

SOURCE

A Yorkshire miner. A locomotive designed by John Blenkinsop is working on the steam-powered wagon way behind him.

Davy

Sir Humphrey Davy (1778–1824) invented a safety lamp in 1815, which could light the mines without setting off explosive gases like 'fire damp' (methane).

Before Davy's invention, mines employed a **fireman**. He went into the mine first, dressed in wet sacking and lying in a hollow covered by planks, pulling a lighted candle on a string through the mineshaft. This set off any pockets of gas before the men started work, using lighted candles to see by. There were many accidents with this system. Generations of miners were grateful for Davy lamps.

2.8 The Industrial Peak?

By the middle of the 19th century, Britain was known as the **'Workshop of the World'**. The economy was based on steam-powered, coal-fuelled, mechanized mass-production in industries as varied as agriculture, textiles, ironware and engineering. British trains and ships provided cheap transport and Britain had one quarter of the world's international trade. Britain basked in confidence.

In 1851, Britain staged the **Great Exhibition** to celebrate the achievements of British and foreign industry. A magnificent exhibition building, over 500 metres long and 125 metres wide and made of iron and glass, was erected in Hyde Park. It was called the **Crystal Palace**. It was open for over five months, included 7,000 British exhibitors and 6,000 from abroad and was visited by over 6 million people. Railway companies brought trainloads from all over the country. The exhibition cost £300,000 to set up, but made a profit of £186,000. This money was used to build the Royal Albert Hall, the Science Museum, the Natural History Museum and the Victoria and Albert Museum.

A SOURCE

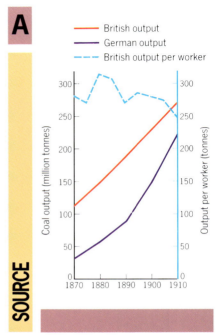

- British output
- German output
- British output per worker

Coal production between 1870 and 1910.

B SOURCE

A mural painting called 'Iron and Steel'. It was painted in 1861 by William Bell Scott at Wallington Hall in Northumberland.

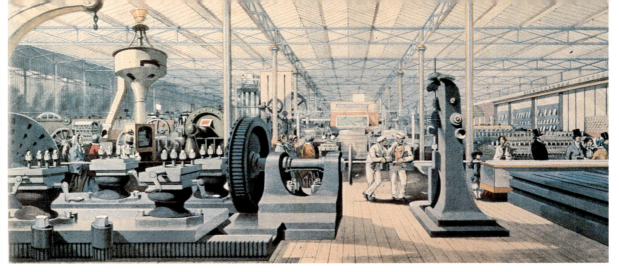

Britain's people benefited from this prosperity. Wages generally rose while prices fell. Consumption of meat, tea, sugar and beer all rose. Many famous retail companies like Cadburys, Boots and Liptons started at this time.

But even at the height of Britain's industrial success, there were danger signs. **Foreign competition** was growing. American and Australian farmers were producing large quanties of grain and meat. Iron and coal industries began to develop in Germany and the United States. Textile industries began to grow in developing countries like India. **Steam cargo ships** brought their goods cheaply to Britain.

These competitors often used **new methods** while the British stayed loyal to the older ones which had been successful for them in the past. Foreign companies adopted electric power; British factories kept steam. Foreign ironmasters used open hearth, then electric arc furnaces; many British ones kept the Bessemer process. Foreign textile producers used automatic looms; the British kept their mules. The new industries of 1900, for example, chemicals and dyes, developed abroad, not in Britain. The Americans and Germans excelled at developing motor cars, while Britain remained the leading producer of trains. By the end of the 19th century, Britain was losing its place as the 'Workshop of the World.'

A Machine Hall at the Great Exhibition of 1851.

Lipton

Sir Thomas Lipton (1850–1931) emigrated to the US in 1865. He worked on tobacco and rice plantations and in a grocer's shop. In 1870, he returned to Glasgow to open a grocer's store of his own; he soon had many more. He was a millionaire by the age of 30. He also ran tea and rubber plantations. Lipton's tea is still famous today. Thomas Lipton was also a keen sailor and tried four times, without success, to win the Americas Cup.

D Year by year the smoke curling from the chimneys of Indian cotton mills increases in volume. It writes the doom of Lancashire.

From an article called 'The Peril of Lancashire' in 'The London Magazine', 1913.

E American ingenuity has undoubtedly taken the lead in making motors of all kinds.

S. S. Wheeler, writing in the 'Illustrated London News' in 1888.

2.9 Transport – Roads

Many of the products of the Industrial Revolution were **heavy** and **bulky**. Grain, wool, iron and coal are examples. Such goods are **difficult** and **expensive** to transport. Other goods, like meat or milk, needed **fast** transport to get them to market while they were still fresh. For all of these reasons, transport was very important during the Industrial Revolution.

In 1750, most people and goods were transported by road on horses, packhorses, carts or stagecoaches. But the roads were in very poor condition. Outside towns, they were usually just tracks created by frequent use. They were muddy in winter and deeply rutted in summer. Since 1555, the law had said that the rich people in each parish had to pay for tools and materials to repair the roads; poorer people had to do six days unpaid work per year on them. But this system did not work.

As the demand for better transport grew, some people saw potential profit in building better roads. They set up groups, called **turnpike trusts**, to run stretches of road like a business. Acts of Parliament gave them permission to charge fees to all the travellers who used certain roads. In return, they would use some of these fees to pay for improvements to the road. They employed expert road builders to repair or replace the old roads. The most famous road-builders were **John Metcalfe**, **Thomas Telford** and **John McAdam**.

A

SOURCE

I left Tonbridge and came to Lewes through the deepest, dirtiest roads in all that part of England. Sometimes a whole summer is not dry enough to make the roads passable. Here I saw a lady drawn to church in her coach by six oxen, the road being so deep and stiff that no horses could go in it.

From 'A Tour Through the Whole Island of Great Britain' (1724) by Daniel Defoe.

This is a scene from a country market town during the coaching era, recorded by Thomas Rowlandson. Note the wide range of road users.

B

SOURCE

C

A crowded stagecoach reaches a toll house. A painting dated 1829.

SOURCE

D SOURCE

The road from Salisbury to Romsey is without exception the finest I ever saw. The trustees of that road deserve all the praise that can be given. It is everywhere broad enough for 3 carriages to pass. Lying in straight lines, with an edge of grass the whole way, it has more the appearance of an elegant gravel walk than a high road.

Arthur Young, commenting on the roads in southern England during his tour of 1768.

McAdam

John Loudon McAdam (1756–1836) was the surveyor of the Bristol Turnpike Trust, caring for the roads in the area. These roads were very busy, and quickly developed potholes. McAdam became famous for finding a cheap way to repair them.

He used gangs of unskilled labourers to break stones into tiny pieces; these were raked and pounded into the potholes. Coach and wagon wheels then crushed the tiny stones into a smooth, solid mass. His road surfaces became so popular that he worked for 107 trusts, repairing 2000 miles of road.

In modern times, macadamized roads are bound together with tar and the surface is called tarmacadam – tarmac for short.

Merchants were glad to pay small fees in exchange for better roads. Stagecoach companies also used them. They could offer much better services on the turnpikes. A journey from London to York took five days in 1750; by 1840 it took only one day. Coaching inns sprang up along the routes to provide food and fresh horses. From 1784, the stagecoaches carried the **Royal Mail**. By 1840, 23,000 people were employed by the turnpike trusts and over 30,000 by the coaching companies.

Eight turnpike trusts were set up between 1700 and 1750 and 55 between 1750 and 1800. By 1830, there were 1,000 turnpike trusts, controlling 23,000 miles of road, about one sixth of the total roads in Britain. But the 'golden age of coaching' came to an end in the 1840s. The next two units explain how canals and railways took the place of long-distance road transport.

2.10 Transport – Canals

Because Britain is an island, a great deal of trade had always been sent by boat along the coasts. Coal from north east England usually came to London by sea. From the ports, barges took goods to inland areas along rivers. Water transport was quicker than road and boats could take heavier loads. But rivers had disadvantages. They meandered and in some places were too shallow for boats to pass. There were many river improvement schemes before 1750. But still rivers flooded in winter and bridges and fords blocked river traffic. Some important industrial areas, such as Birmingham and the Potteries (in Staffordshire) did not have navigable rivers.

In 1757, the **Sankey Brook Canal** was opened. It linked the coalfields around St. Helens to the River Mersey and supplied the people and manufacturers of Liverpool with coal. It was paid for by local businessmen. In 1764, the **Bridgewater Canal**, from Worsley to Manchester, was built by **James Brindley**. The cost of this 10 mile canal was £200,000, paid by the **Duke of Bridgewater**. He owned a coal mine at Worsley and wanted to reduce the cost of taking his coal to Manchester. In 1765, he halved the price of his coal and still made a profit. The Duke also charged other traders to use the canal. He was soon making £80,000 per year in fees.

Other businessmen employed engineers like **James Brindley**, **Thomas Telford** and **William Jessop** to build canals. To raise the money, they set up companies to build the canals, and sold shares in the companies. Shares in the Birmingham Canal Company were first issued at £140 each. The canal was so profitable that its shares sold at £1,170 by 1792.

Part of a letter from the cloth merchants of Wakefield arguing for improvements to the River Calder in about 1700.

— Canals
— Navigable rivers
■ Coalfields

The main canals and navigable rivers of Britain in 1830.

A view of the Regent's Canal at the entrance to Islington Tunnel in 1827. Canals brought grain from the countryside to London and carried its imports from abroad inland.

A good horse on a level railed wagon way can draw only about eight tons, whereas on a canal in a well constructed iron boat it can draw 65 tons in addition to the boat.

A letter to a magazine in 1810. On the roads, it took four horses to carry one ton.

The price of carriage of clay and flint for pottery in Staffordshire, which is 15*s*. (shillings) per ton, will be reduced to 2*s*. The carriage of the earthenware in return will be reduced from 28*s*. to about 12*s*. per ton, which must greatly increase the export of that manufacture.

Josiah Wedgwood, commenting on plans for a canal to link the Rivers Trent and Mersey in 1765. (One shilling = 5p).

Brindley's most famous canal is the **Grand Trunk Canal**, which links the Rivers Trent and Mersey and runs through the Potteries. It was finished in 1777. By 1790, a canal network linked the four major ports of Bristol, Liverpool, Hull and London. Enthusiasm continued. In the 1790s a further 50 canals were built. Some of these were in rural areas and never made great profits for their owners, even though they did bring benefits to the people who lived near them.

The canals provided cheap, reliable transport in the vital early stages of the Industrial Revolution. This was just as important in getting raw materials and fuel to manufacturers and farmers as it was for getting their goods to market. The canals were also useful for transporting breakable goods, like pottery. By 1830, about 40,000 workers were employed on the canals. But by the 1840s the canals were in decline. They had been overtaken by a faster and cheaper form of transport – the railways.

Brindley

James Brindley (1716–72) was an engineer who became Britain's most famous canal builder. He could hardly read or write but was a great solver of practical problems. For the Bridgewater Canal, he built a huge aqueduct to carry the canal over the River Irwell. He also taught his **navvies** (canal workmen) to mix clay, sand and water to make a sticky lining for his canals, to stop the water from seeping away.

2.11 Transport – Railways

In 1750 wagon ways were common in the coalfields. They used horses to pull carts of coal along metal tracks. In 1804, **Richard Trevithick** built a **locomotive**, a steam engine which could pull carts along rails. This was the first railway engine. But it was unreliable; he only built it to demonstrate on a circular track. Others soon followed with improved versions. **William Hedley** built the '**Puffing Billy**' in 1813 to use on the wagon ways of Wylam Colliery. By 1823, there were 20 locomotives moving coal on wagon ways.

Mineowners in Durham decided to build a railed track to take their coal 25 miles from **Stockton to Darlington**. They employed **George Stephenson** to build it. He persuaded them to let him use steam locomotives. In 1825, the line was opened. It took two engines, 'Locomotive No 1' and 'Experiment' to pull 21 coal wagons at eight miles per hour. The railway was soon making a profit. In 1830, Stephenson built another steam railway from **Liverpool to Manchester**. At first, the owners were not sure whether to use horses, locomotives or stationary steam engines pulling carts along with chains. They held the **Rainhill Trials** as a test to help them decide. Stephenson's locomotive the '**Rocket**' won the competition with a speed of 15 miles per hour. When the line opened its trains ran at 40 miles per hour. It was intended to carry trade to and from the port. But by 1850, it was also carrying up to 200,000 passengers per week.

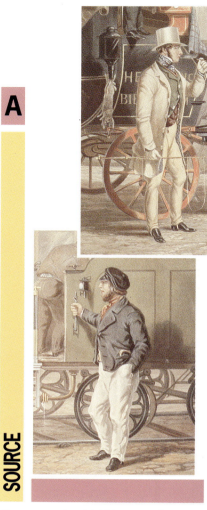

A

SOURCE

Engravings dated 1852, pointedly entitled 'Contrasts – The Driver of 1832 and the Driver of 1852'.

Farmers found railways as useful as manufacturers.

B

SOURCE

The Railway Station' by William Frith, 1862.

C

SOURCE

There were soon so many proposals for new lines that people called it '**railway mania**'. Over 50 schemes were approved by Parliament between 1825 and 1835; in 1836 and 1837, 39 new lines were agreed; and in 1846 alone a further 5,000 miles were started. By 1900, Britain had 22,000 miles of track.

The railways helped **industry** with cheaper carriage of raw materials and finished products. Manufacturers could sell cheaper goods and still make more profit. Railways also bought from industry – iron for rails and locomotives, coal for fuel and bricks for embankments and stations.

Farmers not only got their produce to market cheaper, they could send it further and quicker. This was important for perishable produce like milk and fruit and flowers.

The railways also provided **jobs**. It took 20,000 workers to build the London to Birmingham line. In 1854, there were 90,000 jobs in railway maintenance. Whole new **towns** emerged. Crewe grew from a place with 203 people in 1841 to a railway depot and town with a population of 18,000 in 1871.

As well as cheaper food and goods and more work, there were other public benefits. The mail speeded up; national newspapers flourished; travel became easier. Holidays to seaside towns like Brighton became possible.

At first many people opposed the railways. The coaching and canal companies could not compete with the speed of rail. Some people complained about the pollution; others said that sparks from the engines would burn their crops and the noise would upset farm animals. Some towns, like Northampton and Oxford, refused to let the railways in for several years. But eventually the railways were accepted everywhere. Britain built the world's first rail network and it became a pillar of Britain's success in the mid 19th century.

Stephenson

George Stephenson (1781–1848) is sometimes called 'the father of the railways'. He did not invent the locomotive, but he made 16 of them, and many miles of track; this got businessmen to support the railways. In 1830, crowds came to the opening of his Liverpool to Manchester line. One incident marred the success of the day. To get government support, a minister, William Huskisson, was invited. He stepped in the way of a train and became the world's first railway fatality.

2.12 Transport – Britain Overtaken

Many new methods of transport, apart from railways, developed in the 19th century. Britain did not dominate these. Some were lasting, like **bicycles** and **trams**. Others were less practical, like long- distance balloons and steam-powered cars. The two main developments were in **shipping** and **motor cars**.

In 1845, a new **sailing ship** appeared. It was the American 'Rainbow', the first **clipper**. Clippers were designed to cross the oceans of the world at record speed. Britain's best known clipper was the **Cutty Sark**. Most clippers were American.

Then came **steam-powered ships**. In Scotland, William Symington built a steam-powered riverboat called the '**Charlotte Dundas**' in 1804. A steam ferry called the '**Comet**' was used to take people along the River Clyde from 1812. But it was 1838 before steamships took to the seas. In that year two steamships, the '**Sirius**', an American ship, and the '**Great Western**', a paddle steamer built by **Isambard Kingdom Brunel**, both crossed the Atlantic.

Next came **iron ships**. Brunel's '**Great Britain**' was launched in 1843. In 1881, the '**Servia**' became the world's first ocean-going **steel ship**. It was built in Scotland and could carry 1,250 passengers. Brunel's '**Great Eastern**' was even bigger. It could carry 4,000 passengers. This was the era of the ocean-going passenger liners, dominated by two companies: the American **Cunard Line** and the British **P and O Line**.

B SOURCE

A poster, dated about 1850, advertising the American clipper, 'The Syren'.

C SOURCE

The forests of North America gave the Americans a great advantage in the building of wooden ships. Their huge trade in cotton, timber and grain gave them plenty of business.

From 'Transport 1750–1980' by Simon Mason, 1985.

A SOURCE

'Red Jacket', an American clipper pictured in about 1850.

The luxury P and O liner, 'S.S. Ophir' at Port Said in about 1900.

In 1862, **Etienne Lenoir**, a French engineer, produced a car with a **gas-powered** engine that could run at three miles per hour on roads. It was never a commercial success, but it was the first step towards the mass production of motor cars. Improved versions were developed by **Siegfried Markus**, an Austrian, in 1868, and by **Nikolaus Otto**, a German, in 1876. In 1883, **Gottlieb Daimler**, a manager at Otto's factory, made a **petrol** engine which could be fitted to a car or a bicycle. **Karl Benz**, another German, also produced a motorbike, this one with three wheels, in 1884. By 1885, Benz was selling petrol-driven motor cars. The first British motor car was produced in 1896 by Fred Lanchester. **Rolls-Royce** began manufacturing in 1906. By 1903, there were almost 20,000 cars in Britain, but most of them were foreign.

E

SOURCE

F

SOURCE

The major steps forward in the petrol engine were all made on the continent. Work in this country was hampered by laws passed under pressure from the horse and railway interests to keep steam carriages (cars) off the roads.

From 'An Economic and Social History of Great Britain, 1760–1970' by Trevor May, 1987. (One law passed in Britain in 1865 said that all motorized vehicles on the roads had to keep below four mph and be preceded by a man walking along with a red flag to warn other roadusers).

Brunel

Isambard Kingdom Brunel (1806–59) built the London to Bristol railway, which included the two mile Box Hill tunnel. He designed it so the sun shone through from end to end once a year – on his birthday, 9 April.

Brunel later turned to building ships. His greatest was the iron ship, *Great Eastern*. This ship remained the world's biggest ship for over 40 years. It had a 200 metre hull with a double skin for safety, five funnels and six masts. *Great Eastern* was capable of carrying 4000 passengers at 14 knots (about 16mph).

De Dion car factory, France, c. 1898.

3.1 Trade

Trade was essential to the government which put high taxes on imports to raise money. These taxes also made foreign goods dearer, thus protecting British industries. This is called a **protectionist** trade policy. But British industries also needed foreign trade. They needed imports of raw materials such as cotton, clay and timber. They also needed to export finished products. Selling to the growing population at home was their main income, but the markets abroad provided extra profits. Trade with the Empire was organized for the benefit of Britain. The 17th century **Navigation Laws** forced colonies to buy manufactured goods only through Britain and export their cotton, tobacco, sugar, tea and rice to Britain alone, in British or colonial ships.

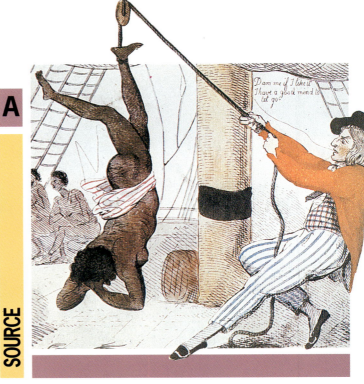

Mistreatment of slaves on the 'middle passage' across the Atlantic was common. It was normal for about a quarter of slaves to die on the journey.

The most profitable trade route in 1750 was the **Triangular Trade**. Ships carrying cloth, pots and pans and guns left Bristol or Liverpool for the west coast of Africa. There, they exchanged their goods for slaves. The slaves were kept in chains below decks in cramped and squalid conditions for the six-week voyage to the West Indies or America. Many died on the way. The remaining slaves were sold and tobacco or sugar bought with the proceeds. These goods were then shipped back to Britain where they were sold at a profit. Then the triangle would start again. The slave trade was abolished in 1807.

By 1840, Britain was the world's leading manufacturer; its industries no longer needed protection. Britain adopted **free trade** policies; the government reduced or abolished taxes on trade. This enabled manufacturers to buy cheaper raw materials; it also encouraged countries who sold Britain raw materials to buy British manufactured products in return. This boosted trade considerably. But soon there were signs of trouble. After 1870 German and American exports began to grow faster than Britain's. Britain's imports grew faster than its exports. The country was spending more than it was earning. Some people began to demand a return to protection to slow down imports.

Wilberforce

William Wilberforce (1759–1833) was a wealthy businessman and the MP for Hull. He was also an evangelical Christian who wanted to reform society. In 1787, he began to campaign for the abolition of slavery.

The first step was achieved in 1807, when it was made an offence for British citizens to take part in the capture and transport of slaves. Wilberforce became ill in 1825. He retired from politics, but he lived long enough to see all slaves in the British Empire set free in 1833.

The dockside in the port of Bristol in the 18th century. The wealthy traders shown in the foreground were useful to new industries as investors. One Gateshead merchant traded in sugar, chocolate, tea and tobacco. He was also the biggest producer of salt in the country and owned coal mines.

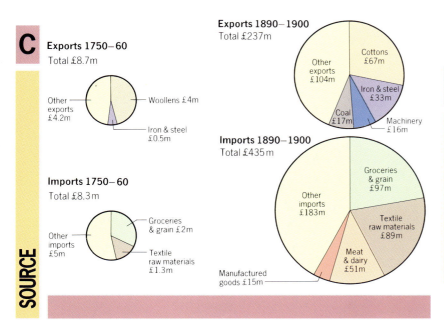

Exports 1750–60
Total £8.7m

Other exports £4.2m
Woollens £4m
Iron & steel £0.5m

Imports 1750–60
Total £8.3m

Other imports £5m
Groceries & grain £2m
Textile raw materials £1.3m

Exports 1890–1900
Total £237m

Other exports £104m
Cottons £67m
Iron & steel £33m
Coal £17m
Machinery £16m

Imports 1890–1900
Total £435m

Other imports £183m
Groceries & grain £97m
Textile raw materials £89m
Meat & dairy £51m
Manufactured goods £15m

British imports and exports (average annual figures for the decades)

You knock over an ornament; picking it up you read on the base, 'Made in Germany'. You jot down your dismal reflections with a pencil made in Germany. You go to bed and glare wrathfully at a picture on the wall of an English village church, and it was 'Printed in Germany'.

From an article, entitled 'Made in Germany,' written in 1896 by E. E. Williams.

3.2 Empire

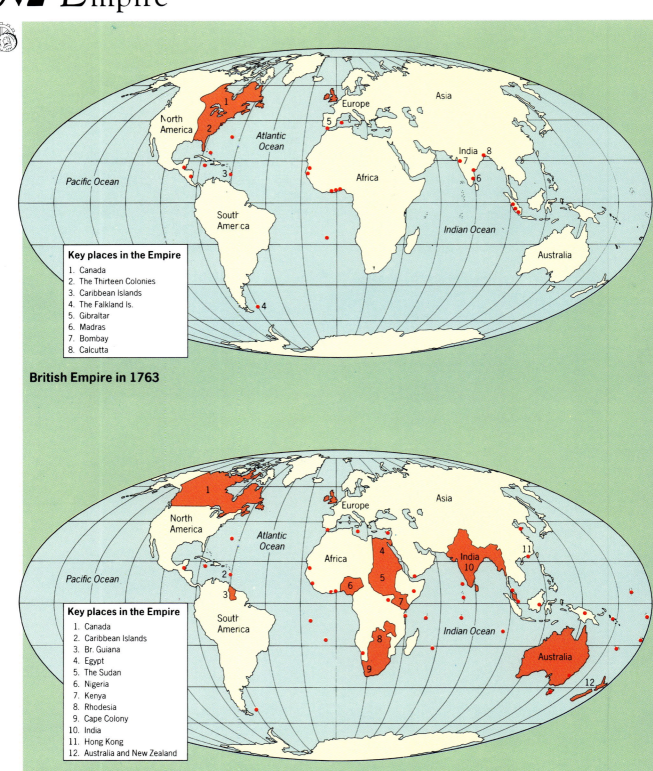

Key places in the Empire

1. Canada
2. The Thirteen Colonies
3. Caribbean Islands
4. The Falkland Is.
5. Gibraltar
6. Madras
7. Bombay
8. Calcutta

British Empire in 1763

Key places in the Empire

1. Canada
2. Caribbean Islands
3. Br. Guiana
4. Egypt
5. The Sudan
6. Nigeria
7. Kenya
8. Rhodesia
9. Cape Colony
10. India
11. Hong Kong
12. Australia and New Zealand

British Empire in 1900

By 1763, Britain was a leading colonial power. Some colonies were the **spoils of war**. In 1713 and 1763, Britain took land in Canada and the West Indies from France. Other colonies were set up by British **settlers**. Britons had been settling in North America, for example, since about 1600. Other British possessions were **trading stations**. The East India Company and the Royal African Company had set up trading posts on the coasts of India, China and Africa.

Over the next century the British Empire grew even bigger. Sometimes, to keep out foreign traders, the trading companies used their private armies to expand inland from their trading posts. This is what happened in India. Later, the **British government** used the army and navy to take over land to prevent countries like France and Germany getting it first. This happened in Africa and New Zealand. Some places, like Gibraltar, were taken as naval bases.

The colonies on the east coast of **America** and the **West Indies** sent sugar, tobacco, cotton and timber to Britain. But in the 1760s arguments broke out with the thirteen colonies in America. The colonists were fed up with interference from a parliament in London which they had no part in electing. They declared their independence in 1776. In the war that followed, the colonists were helped by France and other European countries. The War of American Independence lasted until 1783. The British army was unable to put down the rebellion. The colonies were granted their freedom in 1783 and the United States of America was born.

Britain fared better in **Canada**. In 1759, the British general, James Wolfe, captured the French fortress of Quebec. Cattle and wheat production made this a very prosperous area and many Britons emigrated to Canada. Its population grew to 3 million by 1865 and 6 million by 1900. In 1867 the Dominion of Canada was created, giving Canada more freedom to run its own affairs.

From 'Modern Britain, 1783–1964' by Richards and Hunt.

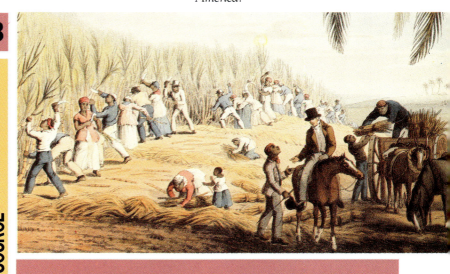

Slaves working on a sugar plantation in the West Indies around 1823. These colonies became even more important after the loss of the thirteen colonies in America.

B

SOURCE

Britain gradually took control of **India**. In 1757, for example, Robert Clive gained Bengal from the French with a private army of the East India Company. Many of the employees of this company lived in luxury and took fortunes in salaries and bribes. Gradually, the British Government took over the powers of the company. The conquest of India continued. In 1857, Indians challenged British control in the Indian Mutiny. This was a rebellion which started amongst the Indians in the British Army. But the revolt was put down and in 1900 India remained firmly under British control. There was no increased freedom for India. Ninety-five percent of the senior jobs in the civil service remained in British hands.

C SOURCE

A British official of the East India Company, attended by his servant, takes a smoke, Indian style (1780). Some British travellers adopted the cultural habits of the countries they visited.

Captain James Cook claimed **Australia** for the British in 1770. They used it as a convict colony from 1788 until 1852. Convicts outnumbered free settlers until 1830. But farming prospered and in 1851 gold was discovered. Emigration from Britain increased; by 1914 Australia had a population of 5 million people and 100 million sheep. **New Zealand** became a British colony in 1840. Farming prospered there too, especially after the development of refrigeration enabled frozen products to be exported to Europe. Australia became a self-governing dominion in 1900 and New Zealand in 1907.

In 1850, Britain's main interests in **Africa** were two strategic areas, Cape Colony in the south and cotton-rich Egypt near the Suez Canal. Between 1880 and 1900 80% of Africa was divided up amongst the European powers. Britain took over control of sixteen colonies including Egypt, the Sudan, Nigeria and Rhodesia. This expansion was sometimes fiercely resisted by local people or settlers. British forces defeated the native Zulus and the Boers (former Dutch settlers) to achieve control of South Africa by 1902.

D SOURCE

A 19th century Australian painting. Settlers in Australia took land from, and even hunted, the Aborigines, who lived there.

The Empire brought **trading benefits** to Britain. The colonies provided cheap supplies of raw materials like cotton, jute, and later rubber, palm oil and nitrates. Wealthier Britons, at least, also enjoyed exotic colonial products like silk, gold, chocolate, rice and tea. Indeed, British culture developed many signs of colonial influence, in food, fashions and buildings. For poorer people, **emigration** to the colonies became one way of escaping unemployment and poor living conditions in Britain. But the colonies eventually caused **trading competition**. Cheap meat and wool from Australia and New Zealand and wheat from Canada were flooding into Britain by 1900.

The **colonies** benefited from British influences in some ways. The British authorities built roads, canals, railways, schools, and hospitals. Some colonies became centres of Christianity. They inherited British laws, language and customs. But the colonies suffered too. British customs were sometimes forced on them and local customs, culture and religions were ignored. This was a factor in causing the Indian Mutiny. Local labour was often exploited; native lands were seized. If there was resistance, the British army usually suppressed it. Some local populations suffered badly. In New Zealand wars and disease reduced the Maori population from about 100,000 in 1815 to 35,000 by 1900.

Cook

Captain James Cook (1728–79) was a navigator and explorer. From 1768–71, and again from 1772–75, he took part in expeditions to explore the southern Pacific.

Cook enforced a diet which included fresh fruit and vegetables on his ships. This prevented **scurvy**, a terrible disease in which blood escapes from the veins, causing ugly swellings all over the body and then death. In 1779, Cook was attacked and killed by natives in Hawaii.

The Royal Pavilion at Brighton, built around 1820, shows the influence of the East on British architects.

E

SOURCE

3.3 Emigration

In 1750, the number of people emigrating was small and roughly balanced by the number of immigrants. This remained true until about 1815. Between 1815 and 1900, 13 million people emigrated from Britain.

There were 'push' and 'pull' causes for emigration. Hardships at home sometimes **pushed** people abroad. Sometimes it was high unemployment, at other times high food prices. Overcrowded living conditions in the towns also persuaded some people to leave. There were two periods of very rapid emigration. One was during the Irish famine which began in 1846; hunger drove 1 million Irish to emigrate by 1850. The other was during the Great Depression in the 1880s when 200,000 people per year were emigrating.

But not all were forced abroad. Sometimes ambition **pulled** people abroad. The discovery of gold in California in 1849, Australia 1851, in the Transvaal in the 1880s and in the Klondike (Alaska) in the 1890s promised huge fortunes to a few dreamers. More realistically, the fertile and cheap land attracted many aspiring farmers to Australia New Zealand and Canada and the booming industries of the East coast of the USA promised rich prospects for the hard working.

B SOURCE

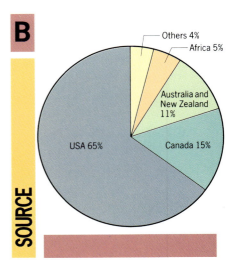

Others 4%
Africa 5%
Australia and New Zealand 11%
USA 65%
Canada 15%

The destination of British emigrants 1820–1900. Towards the end of the century, Australia and New Zealand were growing in popularity.

C SOURCE

FREE EMIGRATION TO SOUTH AUSTRALIA, via Southampton. Free passage to this healthy and prosperous colony to farm workers, shepherds, miners, mechanics and others of good character. The need for labour is urgent and will ensure the comfort of every man and his family.

An advertisement in the 'Northampton Herald', 1846.

A SOURCE

An 1884 painting of immigrants just arrived in New York. Some made a fortune there, like J. J. Astor, who arrived penniless and died with $25 million.

D SOURCE

It cannot be doubted that the removal to Canada and other dominions of boys and girls from our workhouses might do much to relieve the labour market in this country.

From 'The Illustrated London News', 1866.

There was no shortage of encouragement for emigrants. Poor Law guardians and the Salvation Army helped paupers to emigrate; trade unions had emigration funds for their members. The authorities in Australia and New Zealand were desperate for people. Railways and improvements in steam shipping also encouraged emigration by making long distance travel quicker, safer and cheaper than ever before.

A cartoon commenting on the government's policy of encouraging emigration in the 1820s.

SOURCE
E

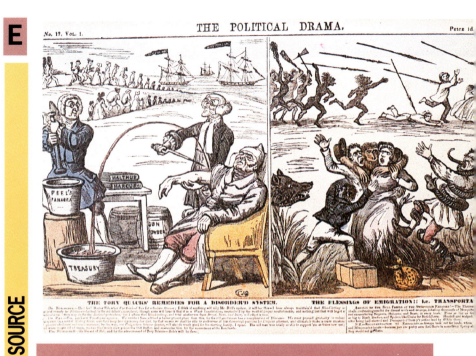

We left Plymouth in February and arrived in Melbourne in June. We had six or seven deaths. Two dear women died in their confinement, one with an inflammation, the rest were children. We had plenty of food, but the little girls' teeth were not strong enough to eat the biscuits. The water got very bad. We found it very hot when crossing the line. We had one gale. Then we got into a cold climate. I was taken ill and was scarcely able to walk when I came on shore.

F

SOURCE

An emigrant writing home from Australia in 1849.

G

Decade	England and Wales	Scotland	Ireland	TOTAL
1830s	100,000	20,000	300,000	420,000
1840s	220,000	60,000	1,110,000	1,390,000
1850s	640,000	183,000	1,231,000	2,054,000
1860s	650,000	158,000	867,000	1,675,000
1870s	1,000,000	200,000	500,000	1,700,000
1880s	1,800,000	300,000	800,000	2,900,000
1890s	1,300,000	200,000	500,000	200,000

SOURCE

Emigration from the United Kingdom.

Astor

John Jacob Astor (1763–1848) was born in Germany. In 1779 he left his poor family farm and travelled to London. Five years later, he emigrated to America. He had almost no money, but started a fur business in New York which became immensely successful. He left a fortune of almost $25,000,000 and a legacy of $350,000 for a new public library in New York. He even had a town, Astoria, named after him.

3.4 Ireland

While the Empire was growing and Britons were emigrating all over the world, Britain was expanding in a different way. In 1801, the **United Kingdom** was formed. Ireland was united to the rest of Great Britain. Links with Ireland had never been happy and this new arrangement was no happier.

In 1750 Ireland was not part of Great Britain. It was a separate country, with its own parliament, but it was ruled from London by the British government. This had been the situation for almost 600 years. But Ireland was not ruled fairly. One reason was religious. Three quarters of the Irish were **Catholic**. Some of Britain's rivals, such as France and Spain, were Catholic. The government didn't trust the loyalty of Catholics, so it repressed them. It made the **Anglican** Church, not the Catholic, the official Irish Church. Catholics were banned from holding high office in government or the armed forces. Catholics were denied land. In 1800, Catholics owned only 15% of the land in Ireland. They had to rent from Protestant, often English, landowners.

In the 1790s, while Britain was at war with France, an Irish rebellion broke out, led by **Wolfe Tone**. The revolt failed, but it convinced the Younger Pitt, the prime minister, that the only way to keep Ireland loyal was to make it part of Great Britain. In 1801 Parliament passed the **Act of Union** which joined Britain and Ireland into the United Kingdom. The Irish got 100 MPs and 32 lords in the British Parliament. Their own parliament in Dublin was abolished.

Still Catholics were refused equality. It took the threat of a rebellion in the 1820s before the Duke of Wellington, the prime minister in 1829, passed the **Catholic Emancipation Act**, which gave equality to Catholics.

A SOURCE

Ireland 1844. There were almost no industries, there were very few towns, and not many farms were large enough to employ labour. It was a country of holdings so small as to be mere patches. The people lived in huts of mud mingled with a few stones, four or five feet high, built on the bare earth, roofed with boughs and turf sods, without chimneys or windows and empty of furniture, where animals and human beings slept together on the mud floor.

From 'The Reason Why', by C. Woodham Smith, 1971.

An engraving of a food riot in Ireland during the famine.

B SOURCE

'The Irish Whiskey Still', a painting by Sir David Wilkie, dated 1840.

In the 1840s, the union was put to the test when **potato blight** ruined the potato crops in Ireland from 1845 to 1849. Farming was undeveloped there; about 2 million people relied chiefly on potatoes for food. Although the British government tried to help, they did not do enough. Shortage of food turned to famine and disease. In the end, 1 million people died and 1.5 million emigrated. Irish opposition to the Act of Union increased still further.

In the 1870s, a terrorist group called the **Fenians** started a campaign of violence against the British. William Gladstone, the prime minister, tried to solve the Irish problems. In 1869, he took away the privileges of the Anglican Church in Ireland. He also passed two Land Acts in 1870 and 1881 to enable the Irish to buy the land they rented. But this was not enough. Inspired by **Charles Parnell**, the Irish demanded independence, or failing that Home Rule (a parliament of their own in Dublin to control domestic affairs). Gladstone tried to pass Home Rule; the Parliament in London overwhelmingly refused.

In 1900 Ireland was still part of the UK and still troubled. Since then, the southern part of Ireland has become an independent country, called Eire. Northern Ireland is still part of the United Kingdom. But the troubles continue.

Parnell

Charles Stewart Parnell (1846–91) led the campaign for Irish Home Rule. He was imprisoned for stirring up Irish unrest in 1881; he encouraged Irish farmers to boycott unfair landlords. He also encouraged Irish MPs to disrupt the work of Parliament with long speeches.

But, in 1890, he had an affair with Mrs Katherine O'Shea. His Catholic support faded; he lost all influence. He died in 1891, five months after marrying her.

4.1 Working Conditions

The changes in industry brought changes in working conditions. Steam-powered machines were used in factories and mills rather than people's homes. This meant large numbers of workers under one roof. Employers often used harsh discipline to organize them. Work in the factories was monotonous, hot and noisy. It could also be dangerous. Few machines had safety guards and fingers and hands could be trapped and mutilated. Industrial processes also had other dangers. Cotton particles or coal dust damaged the workers' lungs. Factories also brought a loss of independence. Cottage workers had worked long hours, but they had been able to work when they pleased and as long as they pleased. This gave them some control over their income. Factory owners demanded regular, long hours and set the levels of pay. Owners employed women and children instead of men if possible. Women were paid half and children one third of a man's wage. This led to exploitation of children. They had always worked from a young age, but usually with their parents.

A SOURCE

Her four year-old child works twelve hours a day with only an interval of a quarter of an hour for breakfast, dinner and tea, and never going out to play.

Report of the Children's Employment Commission, 1843.

B SOURCE

One mode of punishment is to cut off their hair close to the head, especially of those who seem most anxious to preserve it.

An anonymous pamphlet, 1837.

C SOURCE

In Willenhall, the children are most cruelly beaten with a horsewhip, strap, stick, hammer, handle, file or whatever tool is nearest to hand, or are struck with the clenched fist or kicked.

Report of the Children's Employment Commission, 1843.

D SOURCE

I have a belt around my waist, and a chain passing between my legs and I go on my hands and feet. The road is very steep. The pit is very wet. My clothes are wet through almost all day long. The belt is worse when we are in the family way.

Betty Harris, reporting to the Royal Commission on Mining in 1842. She was employed pulling coal tubs underground.

E SOURCE

No man would like to work in a power loom. There is such a clattering it would almost make some men mad; he would have to be subject to a discipline that a hand-loom weaver can never admit to.

A worker giving evidence to a Parliamentary Select Committee in 1835.

F SOURCE

The process of pointing pins on a grindstone can scarcely fail to affect the health of the operator; a portion of the brass dust will reach the mouths and lungs of the grinder; yet he employs no precautions.

A visitor to a Birmingham metal works in 1844.

G

A painting entitled 'The Wounded Workman'. Between 1856 and 1866, 1,000 miners died from accidents every year.

H

SOURCE

Our only advantages consist in cheap machinery and low rates of interest. By restricting mills, we give up these advantages and hand them over to the enemy.

'The Factory Questions Considered' by Robert Hyde Greg, 1837.

I

SOURCE

Extreme hardship would be inflicted upon tens of thousands of families in Lancashire and Yorkshire by a law fixing the hours at eight or even ten hours and absolutely forbidding the employment of a child for a minute longer.

'The Leeds Mercury', December 1831.

Nobody expected the Government to interfere at first. In 1750, governments were expected to keep the country's finances healthy and control foreign policy. In social affairs, they adopted a policy of **laissez-faire**, leaving things alone to work themselves out. Working conditions were seen as a private arrangement between employers and workers. Many people felt that restrictions on employers could harm profits; reduced hours for children might cause financial hardships to some families.

In the 1820s, some humanitarian factory owners, such as Robert Owen and John Fielden, appealed to the government to act. They were supported by a few MPs, like Michael Sadler. The best known campaigner was **Lord Anthony Ashley Cooper** (later **Earl of Shaftesbury**). He was one of a group of evangelical Christians who campaigned against the evils of society. They pressed for a maximum 10 hour working day. The government set up a series of enquiries in response to this campaign. When the official reports showed how bad working conditions were, Parliament and the public were shocked. Laws were passed to force improvements. Most famous are the **Factory Act** of 1833 and the **Mines Act** of 1842. The laws gradually protected more and more workers and inspectors were appointed to enforce them.

Shaftesbury

Anthony Ashley Cooper (1801–85), Lord Ashley, later became Lord Shaftesbury. He led the 'Ten Hours Movement' to limit the working day and helped apprentices, mine workers and 'climbing boys' who were sent up chimneys to clean them. He was on the Board of Health set up in 1848 to improve living conditions and was President of the Ragged Schools Union for poor chidren.

4.2 Living Conditions ✓

After 1750, the population rose rapidly. London and the industrial towns grew fastest. Between 1801 and 1851, Glasgow's population grew from 75,000 to 350,000. Houses were squeezed into the centres of towns or around the factories. Landlords crammed as many people into houses as they could.

The **water supply** was another problem. Rivers were the main source of water for drinking, cooking and washing. In London's Highgate, water was purchased by the bucketful from stand-pipes in the street; at Hyde, Manchester, people paid one shilling (5p) per week to buy water from carts. Only the water companies were happy with this situation.

Sewage and rubbish was left in back yards, piled up at the end of the street or thrown into open drains which ran down the roads. Even where there were drains and sewage pipes, they normally ran into the local rivers – where people collected their water. In London, the Battersea sewer emptied into the Thames just above the Chelsea water intake.

Rapid population growth caused urban squalor in all the great cities of Europe. This is a scene from the streets of Paris in 1892.

A SOURCE

The working classes of Liverpool numbered 160,000. Of these, 22,158 lived in cellars (underneath other people's houses).

Extract from the 1841 Census Report.

B SOURCE

We prefer to take our chance with the cholera than be bullied into health. There is nothing a man hates so much as being cleansed against his will.

'The Times', 1854, arguing against public health reform.

C SOURCE

Disease thrived in these conditions. The water carried germs; the rubbish and sewage attracted flies; the crowded rooms spread lice. The most common diseases were smallpox, scarlet fever, typhus, typhoid and tuberculosis. In 1831, a new one was added: **cholera** arrived from the continent. There were further outbreaks in 1838, 1848 and 1854. These were not only diseases of the urban poor. Wealthier people often had running water in their houses. But it came from the same rivers. Prince Albert, Queen Victoria's husband, died of typhoid. Country people avoided the overcrowding, but their cottages were often even more cold and damp.

E SOURCE

A cartoon from 1828, showing the state of London's river water. It was entitled 'Monster Soup'. Cholera was carried in infected water. In 1849, 16,000 Londoners died of cholera.

The principle of **laissez-faire** discouraged government action to improve living conditions. MPs didn't see it as their business to interfere. But after a campaign by **Edwin Chadwick**, in 1848, the Central Board of Health was set up. This suggested ways to prevent disease in the towns. Local boards were set up in large towns to carry out the instructions. In 1875, the **Public Health Act** made local councils responsible for public health. They had to keep pavements lit, paved and cleaned, sewers clean, and refuse clear from the streets. They raised the necessary funds from ratepayers. Another reform passed in 1875 was the **Artisans' Dwellings Act**. This gave councils power to clear slums and build better houses for working people. Improvements in medicine also made living conditions better. By 1900, **vaccines** had been found to prevent many infectious diseases.

Hill

Octavia Hill (1838–1912) set up a school in London for poor children. Later she borrowed money to buy and improve three local houses to provide homes for the poor. The success of this led to many more London housing developments. She was also concerned about preserving open spaces in towns and was a co-founder of the National Trust in 1895.

D

SOURCE

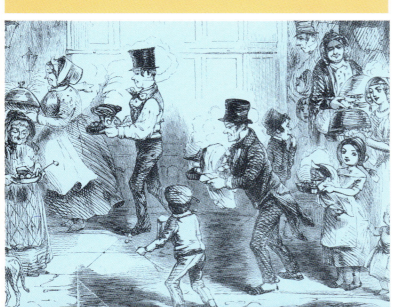

Some poor people could not afford a stove or coal to cook over. Even those who could, might not have clean water for cooking. Many people took their food to the local baker to cook.

4.3 The Poor and Paupers

In 1750, most of the British population were **poor**. They had too little for a comfortable life. Historians disagree about whether working people became better off during the Industrial Revolution. Everyone agrees that the average standard of living rose from 1850 to 1900 as the economy boomed and food prices fell. But what about 1750–1850?

Unemployment or low wages made some people **destitute**: too poor to survive without help. These people were called **paupers**. The **Old Poor Law** said that every parish had to raise money from the ratepayers to support its paupers. In 1750, paupers were treated in various ways. Young paupers could be made apprentices with local craftsmen. Older paupers could be given useful work or put in a workhouse. In 1795, the parish of **Speenhamland** in Berkshire decided to give paupers **money**. The amount depended on the pauper's income and the price of bread.

By about 1830, the Old Poor Law needed reform. It was very expensive. It varied too much between parishes. Ratepayers said that the Speenhamland system made people lazy and encouraged them to rely on help from the parish. Workers said it encouraged employers to pay low wages. In 1830 there were riots over the south of England, called the Swing Riots. Some people thought the Speenhamland system was to blame.

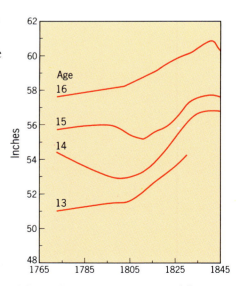

Marine Society measurements of the height of naval recruits, 1770–1845.

A picture of the poverty of 'Farmer Giles', by William Heath in 1829. The farmer's note says: 'This is to inform you that the children have been received into the Workhouse.'

Chadwick

Edwin Chadwick (1800–90) was a social reformer. He was the Secretary to the Poor Law Board. At the time, workhouses were called 'bastilles' (after the French prison) and were so hated by the poor that Chadwick became very unpopular. His job showed him the terrible living conditions of the poor. He wrote the *Report on the Sanitary Conditions of the Labouring Population*, which was the main cause of the 1848 Public Health Act, which began to improve living conditions in towns.

In 1834, the **Poor Law Amendment Act** was passed. It said that crippled or sick paupers should not be blamed for their problems. They should get **outdoor relief** – money or food in their own homes – or special homes should be built to look after them. But **able bodied** paupers should be sent into **workhouses**. Workhouses were made harsher than the worst conditions outside. Families were separated. Work was hard and monotonous, for example stone breaking or bone crushing. Uniforms had to be worn at all times, smoking and alcohol were forbidden and punishments for misbehaviour were harsh. The diet was enough to keep people alive but was kept uninteresting. This **New Poor Law** was still in force in 1900.

A London workhouse in 1809. What similarities did it have with workhouses after 1834?

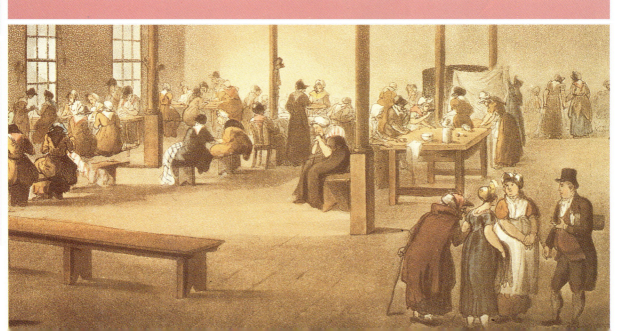

4.4 Law and Order

In 1750, **crime** was rife in Britain's cities. Pickpockets and footpads robbed people in the streets, highwaymen infested the roads. There was no proper police force. Every parish had a constable, untrained and underpaid; some had watchmen to patrol the streets at night. The army could be called upon to put down riots. There were few prisons. These were regarded as places to keep people awaiting trial, not places to punish or reform criminals. The main means of preventing crime was to deter criminals with harsh punishments. **Transportation** to the colonies was common. In 1750, over 150 crimes were punished by **death**. These included shoplifting goods worth more than 5s. (25p), stealing a sheep and even damaging Westminster Bridge. Execution was by **public hanging**. Hangings were a popular form of entertainment; 28 people were killed in a crush at a Newgate hanging in 1802.

Between 1750 and 1820, crime got worse. Reported crimes rose from 35,000 for the period 1810 to 1817 to 65,000 from 1817 to 1824. The rapidly growing and overcrowded cities, periods of economic depression and high food prices during the wars against France (1793–1815) all contributed to this. But in 1820, London had only 300 parish constables for over 1 million people.

Sir Robert Peel, Home Secretary in the 1820s, decided to make changes. First, he reformed the **penal code**. He took 100 crimes off the list punished by death. By 1837 capital punishment was only used for murder, attempted murder and treason. But what would replace hanging as a deterrent to crime?

SOURCE A

When she returned, a loaf of bread, a piece of bacon, about 2lbs of cheese and a gown had been taken away. She went for a constable. George Morris owned up to the deed. He merely did it from want. Sentence, 7 years transportation.

From *All Stretton parish records*.

SOURCE B

Those condemned to the rope are placed on a cart, each with a rope about his neck. The cart is driven off under the gallows. Then the criminals' friends come and draw them down by the feet so that they might die all the sooner.

From *'Travels in England' by Thomas Platter, 1799*.

SOURCE C

The executions have little effect in stopping crimes. It is not so much the harshness as the certainty of punishments which puts criminals off. Robbers bear in mind the numbers of thieves whom juries will not convict because they are unwilling to hang men for a trivial act of theft.

Sir John Fielding, 1776.

SOURCE D

It is difficult to imagine both an efficient police force and a perfect freedom of action for the people of this country. We all value the lack of interference in our daily lives and to lose this at the expense of a lower crime rate is too much of a sacrifice.

'The Times' in 1822.

SOURCE

This cartoon, dated 1856, jokingly suggested anti-strangling clothes for the streets.

Fry

Elizabeth Fry (1780–1845) was a committed Christian who took pity on the women and children in Britain's gaols. In 1816, she set up a school in Newgate Gaol, in London, for reading, writing and sewing. She used religious readings to encourage women to live a better life. This was in contrast to the normal practice of treating prisoners cruelly to deter them from crime. Fry's example changed attitudes all over Europe.

In 1829, Peel founded the **Metropolitan Police Force** in London. The force had 3000 constables. He armed them only with truncheons and gave them non-military blue uniforms because many people were worried about the government using the police to rule the country by force. This still left problems elsewhere. In 1834, Liverpool had only 50 nightwatchmen to keep order in a city of 250,000. But new laws allowed cities, from 1835, and then counties, from 1839, to set up their own police forces. Crime declined slowly and the police were used to disperse demonstrations peacefully in place of the army.

These changes meant that more people were sent to **prison**. The prisons were crowded; 'gaol fever' (typhus) was rampant and prisoners had to pay gaolers for decent food and bedding. **John Howard** and **Elizabeth Fry** campaigned for improvements. In 1823, Peel had passed the **Gaols Act**. This insisted on paid warders, women warders for women prisoners, prison chaplains and doctors and the abolition of prisoners' fees. In 1835, prison inspectors were appointed and 50 new gaols were built by 1850. But prison conditions remained harsh. In London's Pentonville Prison, built in 1842, prisoners had to be silent at all times, wear masks so that other prisoners could not recognise them and work from 6am until 7pm. Prisons were still overcrowded in 1900.

Prisoners were usually given useless work to do. This is the treadmill at Brixton Prison, London. In the 1840s, some prisoners climbed the equivalent of 2,500 metres per day.

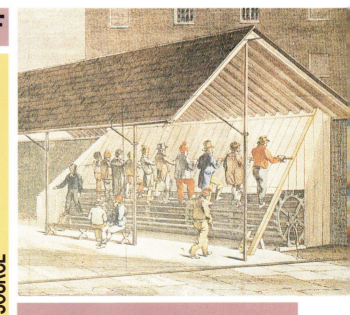

SOURCE

4.5 Education

In 1750, the wealthy sent their sons to **public schools**. There were nine of these; Eton and Harrow are the best known. There were no public schools for girls until after 1850. There were also about 100 fee paying **grammar schools**. Some boys went on to university. There were only two of these in England: Oxford and Cambridge; Scotland had four.

For poor children there were **dame schools**. These charged low fees, but they were often only somewhere for parents to leave children; they gave little education. There were also **charity schools**, like those run by the Society for the Propagation of Christian Knowledge. **Sunday schools** began after 1780 when Robert Raikes formed a Sunday school in Gloucester to give religious teaching to boys and girls.

The rise in the population after 1750, especially in the towns, made it obvious that there should be more schools. The government would not provide any, so the the Church of England founded the **National Society** in 1811 to provide schools for Anglican boys and girls. In 1814, the Nonconformist churches set up the **British and Foreign Schools Society**. These church societies used money raised by charity and charging small fees to build schools and employ teachers. **Ragged schools** – free schools, with very basic lessons, set up by individuals as acts of charity for the very poor – existed by 1844.

Augustus Hare (1848), remembering his time at Harrow School.

Like the public schools, Oxford and Cambridge concentrated on Latin and Greek. No science departments were founded until about 1850. Many students, like these, wasted their time instead of studying.

B SOURCE

Present 170 boys; the room wil hold 400. The only book in use for the upper classes was the Bible There were no maps in the school. The children were taught nothing either of History or Geography. Indeed the master could not find time to give any direct instruction to the school, but was obliged to depend on his little monitors, not one of whom was 12 years old.

A government report on a church society school. The teacher was using the monitorial system, whereby he taught monitors and they taught the rest of the class.

C SOURCE

SOURCE D

It would teach them to despise their lot in life instead of making them good servants. It would enable them to read seditious pamphlets, vicious books and publications against Christianity; it would render them insolent to their superiors.

Davies Giddy MP, in 1807, speaking in Parliament against education for the poor.

SOURCE E

On the provision of education depend our industrial prosperity, the safe working of the constitution and our national power. If we are to hold our position among the nations of the world, we must make up for the smallness of our numbers by increasing the intellectual force of the individual.

E. W. Forster MP, in 1870.

SOURCE G

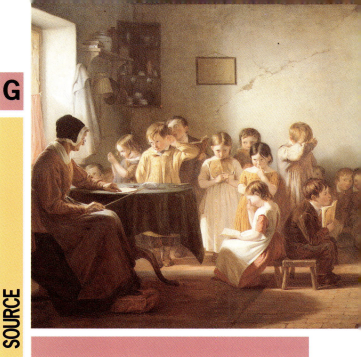

A dame school from a mid-19th century painting. Many women who ran dame schools had other jobs which they did as well.

Eventually, schools were helped by Government. In **1833**, the government agreed to give an **annual grant** of £20,000 to the two church societies. The grant increased until, by 1858, it had reached £600,000 per year. But there were still areas where there were too few schools. **Forster's Education Act** of 1870 gave ratepayers the chance to elect local school boards to provide extra schools. Elementary education became compulsory up to the age of ten in 1880 and free from 1891.

SOURCE F

Lancaster

Joseph Lancaster (1778–1838) ran a school in Southwark. He created the **monitorial system**, in which a teacher instructed a small number of **monitors** who then taught the rest of the class. Under this system, £300 could finance a school for a thousand pupils. Andrew Bell created a similar system at the same time. Bell became the adviser of the National Society. Lancaster advised the British and Foreign Schools Society. Their methods influenced teaching throughout the century.

A London museum in 1845. Many people relied upon libraries, museums and evening classes to make up for the poor schooling they had received.

4.6 Religion

Before 1750, the Church was a centre of the community. People tended to be baptized, married and buried at the same church; attendance at church was high. But the Church of England was in decline in 1750. Partly this was due to the **population increase**. Especially in the growing towns, people lost touch with their Church. The clergy couldn't know everyone in their congregations. But the problem was also partly to do with the structure in the Church itself. The clergy were often appointed because of political or family connections. Some parsons didn't live in their parishes; some held posts in several parishes. The middle and upper classes stayed loyal to the Church. But for many their religion was now a code of respectable behaviour rather than faith. However, there were two great religious revivals.

Methodism was the work of **John Wesley**, who began as a Church of England minister in 1725. He preached the simple virtues of purity and honesty to the poor in the industrial areas. His sermons promised paradise to his followers, and he used rousing hymns. He took people beyond the poverty and pain of their daily lives. Wesley encouraged people to respect good behaviour, not rank. This was resented by the Anglican (Church of England) bishops. They barred him from preaching in their churches. For a long time Wesley held his services in the open air. But in 1784 he began to separate his Methodists from the Church of England. He died in 1791. There were about 250,000 Methodists in Britain by 1815.

A cartoon by Rowlandson commenting on the state of the Church of England whose clerics grew fat while poor people starved.

An 1851 print of John Wesley preaching a sermon.

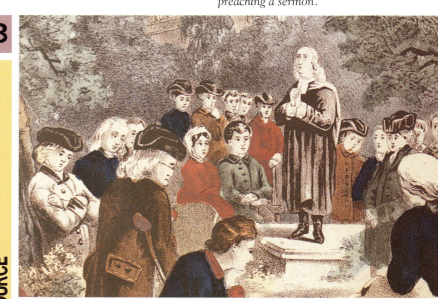

A second revival of religious fervour arose in the form of the **Evangelicals**. These were Christians who, from about 1780, decided to put their religious convictions to work by attacking un-Christian features of society. Most notable amongst the early Evangelicals was **William Wilberforce**. His campaigns led to the abolition of the slave trade. Another famous Evangelical campaigner was the **Earl of Shaftesbury**. He helped the Ten Hour Day Movement in the 1830s, piloted the the Mines Act of 1842 through Parliament, served on the Public Health Board 1848–52, was President of the Ragged Schools Union for poor children, and helped improve the working conditions of apprentice chimney sweeps. Other Evangelical campaigners were **Michael Sadler** who worked for factory reform and **Elizabeth Fry** who promoted prison reforms. In 1878 Charles Booth founded the **Salvation Army**; its bright uniforms, brass bands and direct approach appealed to working people. It has flourished and performed good works all over the world.

The Church of England also improved the quality of its clergy and began a building programme. Many of our town churches date from about 1850. Despite this, when the first **Religious Census** was taken in 1851 it revealed a shock. Not much more than a third of the population went to church on Sundays.

Scientific research may have contributed to the move away from church-going. Discoveries in geology had made it quite clear that the Earth had not been created in six days in the way the Bible described. In 1859, **Charles Darwin's** 'Origin of Species' argued that human beings were not the special creation of God, but had evolved from simpler forms of life. Although Britain remained a country whose culture was dominated by Christian ideals, the number of practising Christians had become a minority.

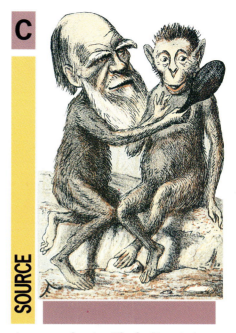

C SOURCE

A cartoon showing Charles Darwin in 1874. His explanation of the origins of human life undermined the teaching of the Church.

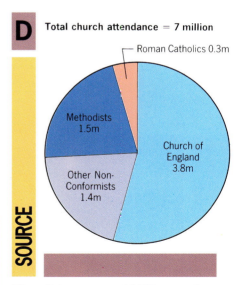

D SOURCE

Total church attendance = 7 million

Roman Catholics 0.3m

Methodists 1.5m

Church of England 3.8m

Other Non-Conformists 1.4m

The religious census of 1851 counted all those who went to church on Mothering Sunday. The total population of England and Wales was 18 million. Assuming that 30 per cent would be too young or ill to attend, about 12.5 million could have been at church that day.

Booth

William Booth (1829–1912) believed that London's poor were driven to sin by poverty. In 1878 he founded the Salvation Army. It was organized on a military basis, with coloured uniforms, marching bands and Booth as its general. Women worked equally alongside men. They went into the poorest areas to explain their religious beliefs and set up over 30 relief centres providing food, shelter and training for the poor.

5.1 Power to the People (1)

After 1750, the Industrial Revolution and the growth of the British Empire changed life in Britain. For example, it created a wealthy new middle class of merchants and industrialists. It also created towns teeming with working people crushed together in greater numbers than ever before. Some of these changes pleased people. But other changes caused grievances. People with grievances turned to their employers or the government to solve their problems. Thus the **social** and **economic** changes became **political** issues.

In 1750, few working- or middle-class people had the vote. If they wanted change they could not vote for new MPs who could raise their cause in Parliament. But there was plenty they wanted to change – government trading policies, working conditions, living conditions, high food prices or unemployment. Their protests took various forms but they were rarely successful.

Some working class people resented new machines which replaced skilled jobs, like hand-loom weaving. From 1811–12 there was a widespread outbreak of machine breaking by hundreds of workers known as the **Luddites** in the North. An employer was killed at Huddersfield and a factory burned down in Wigan. In 1830, there were similar attacks on farm machinery all over southern England in the **Swing Riots**. The government used troops to put down machine breaking. In 1830, nineteen people were hanged and 457 transported.

On 20 April a major fight took place at Middleton, where Daniel Burton's power-loom mill was attacked by several thousands. The mill was assailed by showers of stones and its defenders replied with musket-fire, killing three and wounding more. The army then met them and killed at least seven.

A newspaper report from 1812. The loom breaking was supposed to have been led by a man called Ned Ludd, but he probably did not exist.

The House of Commons in about 1800. MPs were almost all wealthy landowners. They feared a revolution like the one in France in 1789.

B SOURCE

C SOURCE

A cartoon from 1819, showing the Peterloo Massacre.

Hunt

Henry 'Orator' Hunt (1773–1835) was a wealthy farmer with a wild background. He eloped with a friend's wife and was imprisoned for assault. He wanted the vote for all men and became a well known radical speaker. He was six foot tall and wore a white top hat. He had a bellowing voice. It was said that when he was furious; a contemporary said that:

his eyes were blood-streaked and started from their sockets.

Sometimes, middle and working-class people joined together in demonstrations. In 1819, a mass meeting was held in St Peter's Fields, Manchester. It was to be non-violent. Thousands of men women and children came with banners flying demanding 'Votes for All' and 'A Free Press.' Half-way through, the magistrates decided that the meeting was illegal and sent a troop of cavalry in to arrest 'Orator' Hunt, the main speaker. Angry protesters barred the way. The soldiers drew their sabres; there was general panic. In ten minutes the field was cleared, but 400 people, including 113 women, were wounded and 11 killed. People called it '**Peterloo**', a sarcastic reference to the famous Battle of Waterloo of 1815.

In 1820, there was a plot, called the Cato Street Conspiracy, to overthrow the government. This picture shows government officers bursting in on the plotters. The leaders were executed.

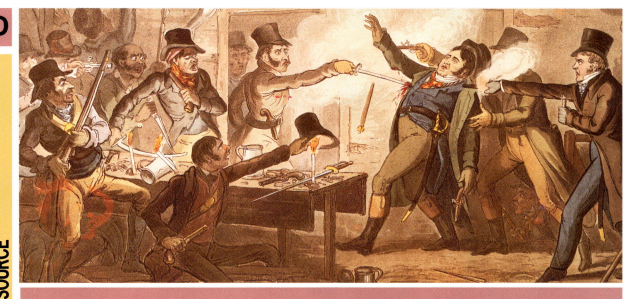

D SOURCE

5.2 Power to the People (2)

The big question from 1830 to 1850 was who had the vote. In 1831, there were 16.4 million people in Britain. Only 478,000, all men, could vote. They voted for 558 MPs of whom 400 were elected by boroughs (towns). But these towns had been chosen between the middle ages and 1600. By 1830, many of these boroughs were tiny. 50 of them had fewer than 40 voters; Appleby in Cumbria had one voter. Some huge new towns, like Manchester, had no MPs.

This was so unfair that the smallest boroughs were called 'rotten boroughs'. There was no secret voting, so landlords could bribe or threaten voters into voting for their candidates. The House of Commons was full of wealthy landowners. The working people and even the middle classes had few MPs to speak for them. By 1830, demands for reform of Parliament had been building for 50 years. The government was frightened that there would be a revolution if they refused any longer. In 1832, the Great Reform Act was passed. It changed the rules about who could vote; it took MPs away from the smallest boroughs and gave MPs to the towns. The electorate, the people who could vote, almost doubled, to about 815,000.

A cartoon from 1832 showing the government chopping down the rotten boroughs. The Reform Act took away MPs from 86 tiny boroughs and gave them to the big towns.

B

SOURCE

58

It is safe to say that the Act did nothing for the working classes, in spite of their enthusiastic support for reform. It was the factory owners rather than the factory workers who benefited. Only about 400,000 new voters were added. In other words, the landed gentry had merely shared a little of its political power with the new industrial and commercial middle class.

From 'Britain Since 1700' by R.J. Cootes, 1968.

1832 was a turning point in British history. It opened the way for social reforms over the next few years. It began a long period of middle class control of Parliament. It set the precedent for later Reform Acts which gave the vote to workers in 1867 and the whole adult population by 1928. Its greatest service to the British people was to prevent a revolution.

From 'A Survey of British History' by C.P. Hill, 1968.

After 1832, the working classes were desperately disappointed that they still did not have the vote. They were not pleased by the reforms passed by the new Parliament, like the New Poor Law. They started a campaign for six new changes to the system for electing MPs. These 'Six Points' made up the **'People's Charter'**. Supporters of the Charter – known as Chartists, wanted votes for all men, secret voting, payment of MPs, equal constituencies, annual elections and freedom for anyone to stand as an MP. The Six Points were intended to give working people influence in Parliament.

The supporters of the Charter tried several ways of getting Parliament to accept it. Some people wanted to take over the country by force and then put the Charter into practice. In 1839, for example, there was an uprising in Newport, Wales. Other people wanted to persuade Parliament. In 1839, 1842 and 1848, huge petitions were presented to Parliament. In 1848 there was a big rally in London to take the final petition, with its five million signatures, to Westminster.

O'Connor

Feargus O'Connor (1794–1855) was a rousing speaker and journalist, who described the upper class as 'the big-bellied, little-brained, numbskull aristocracy'. For a while he was the most popular Chartist leader and was known as 'the People's Champion'. But he was a poor leader, less reliable than William Lovett, his main rival. His land scheme for settling the poor from the towns on their own farms was a financial failure. He later became mentally ill and died in a mental asylum.

But the Charter was never adopted by Parliament. Its demands were too extreme for most people at that time to accept. Once Parliament refused, there was no support amongst working people for a revolution to force the Charter on Parliament. Power stayed in the hands of the middle and upper classes.

The Chartists taking their petition to Parliament in 1842.

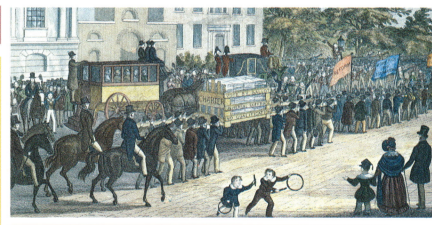

5.3 Power to the People (3)

After 1850 the working class gained more political influence. Their first successes were with **New Model Trade Unions**. These were unions for skilled workers. They charged fairly high subscriptions which were used to provide benefits like sickness and unemployment payments to their members. They were very moderate. They didn't threaten to destroy industry, they negotiated with employers for improvements. There were very few strikes. By 1865 one such union, the Amalgamated Society of Engineers, had 30,000 members.

Union leaders began to meet politicians to argue that working men should have the vote. The new political leaders, like **William Gladstone**, a Liberal, and **Benjamin Disraeli**, a Conservative, could see that working people could be trusted with a share of power. They were impressed by their organization and moderation. In 1867, the Tory government passed the **Second Reform Act**.

This Act increased the electorate from about 1.5 million to about 2.5 million. The new voters were the better off workers in the towns. In 1872, the Ballot Act was passed by the Liberal Party. This made voting secret; it was now possible for people to vote without worrying about threats from their landlords or employers. In 1884 the Third Reform Act gave more working people the vote. The electorate rose to about 5 million out of a population of 30 million. Parliament now had to listen to the needs of the working class. New laws, such as the **Public Health Act** of 1875, improved their living conditions.

But there were still many working people without the vote. They needed another way to make their voices heard. This led to the **New Unions**. These were trade unions for unskilled labourers, like dockers and railway workers. They had low subscriptions, and they weren't interested in side benefits.

A SOURCE

Every man who is not incapacitated by some personal unfitness or political danger is morally entitled to come within the pale of the constitution.

Gladstone's attitude to the vote in 1864.

B SOURCE

His virtue, prudence, intelligence and frugality entitle him to enter the privileged pale of the constituent body of the country.

Disraeli describing the skilled working class in 1860.

C SOURCE

A New Model Union membership card. It tells us a lot about the image of the skilled working classes by 1870.

I do not believe in sick pay, out of work pay and other pays. The thing to do is firstly to organize, then reduce hours of labour and that will prevent illness and members out of work.

Will Thorne, leader of the Gas Workers' Union, 1889.

Besant

Annie Besant (1847–1933) was an early British socialist. In 1875, she was prosecuted for advocating birth control for women.

In 1888, Annie Besant organized a strike for more pay and better working conditions for women at the *Bryant and May* matchworks in London. These women earned just one penny a week making matches using phosphorus on the head. Phosphorus caused an illness called 'phossy jaw'. The strike was the first success for the New Unions.

'The British Beehive' an 1840 engraving re-issued in 1867 as part of the campaign for the 1867 Reform Act. It has a clear message about British society by the middle of the 19th century.

They set out to *force* employers to increase wages. The dockers' strike forced an increase in pay in 1889. By 1900 there were 2 million members of New Unions.

These unions began to work with the few working class MPs, like **Keir Hardie**. They wanted a stronger voice in Parliament for the working class. In 1900, they formed the **Labour Representation Committee** to help working class candidates for Parliament. In 1906, 29 LRC candidates were elected. They decided to call themselves the **Labour Party**.

By 1900 the monarch had very little real power. The landowners still dominated the House of Lords and provided many government ministers, but they shared power in the Commons with the middle classes. Many working men also had the vote as well as the support of unions and the Labour Party. Women still had no say in politics.

E

A PENNY POLITICAL PICTURE FOR THE PEOPLE,
WITH A FEW WORDS UPON PARLIAMENTARY REFORM.
BY THEIR OLD FRIEND, GEORGE CRUIKSHANK

6.1 Britain in 1900

After 1750, Britain had the world's first industrial revolution. By 1900 it was still the most powerful industrial and trading nation, though others were catching up fast. Steam powered machinery had increased output and changed working conditions. Some old skilled crafts had disappeared. The population had grown from 7 to 37 million. The extra people provided the demand and the workers for industry and had created huge industrial cities like Manchester, Glasgow and Birmingham. They had thousands of factories and millions of crowded terraced houses. Gradually, they got water supplies, sewerage, schools and churches too. Farmers had found ways of producing enough food to feed the cities, using fewer workers. Horse power had been joined by steam power and petrol.

During this time, too, Britain tried to create a new relationship with Ireland; lost its American colonies; and gained the biggest empire in the world. Britain exported more than any other nation, including over 13 million Britons (the equivalent of 20% of the whole population of Britain today), who emigrated abroad. Imperial rivalry was causing friction between Britain, France and Germany.

'Work' an 1863 painting by Ford Madox Brown. The Victorians saw hard work as a virtue. This painting makes the point that the townspeople, the bookish gentlemen looking on, the children and even the poor street seller all depend on the work of the six heroic navvies at the centre of the painting.

A

SOURCE

By 1900 many British people enjoyed travelling by railway to the seaside, with its jellied eels, bathing machines and Punch and Judy on the beach. They might visit a travelling circus or, in the evenings, one of the music halls that existed in all the major towns. Public houses flourished, horse racing, cricket and boxing were at least as popular as they had been a century before and had been joined by league soccer, the greatest of all mass sports. Cock-fighting and badger-baiting continued in the 1880s but the RSPCA was campaigning against them. Thomas Hardy, Emily Bronte and Charles Dickens were great Victorian authors; Bernard Shaw and Oscar Wilde playwrights; Constable and Turner artists.

By 1900 it was possible to send telegrams to America through a trans-Atlantic cable laid in 1865 and to speak on the telephone, invented in 1876. Gramophones first appeared in 1877, and radios in 1896. Dynamite and machine guns had been around since 1867, typewriters since 1874, and the first movies since 1895. Doctors used blood transfusions, anaesthetics, like chloroform, and antiseptics, like carbolic acid, though penicillin and the National Health Service were still almost 50 years away. People opened tins of Heinz food from America, or possibly asked their cooks, maids or butlers to.

By 1900 the first primitive electric vacuum cleaners, kettles, washing machines and dishwashers had arrived. Yet 20,000 homeless people lived in London's streets. Amelia Bloomer had designed the first trousers for women in 1862, but they still could not vote. Men were wearing top hats; but underclothes were still rare among the poor. Some streets were lit with gas or electric lights. Finally, as befits a year which sits astride the old Britain and the new, London in 1900 had thousands of new petrol driven motor buses but Londoners also used 116,000 horses which produced almost half a million tons of manure a year.

B

SOURCE

TOO MUCH OF A GOOD THING

EVERY VARIETY OF PLEASURE RESORT.

PARKS & PLAYGROUNDS
RIVER-SIDE
COUNTRY-SIDE
SEASIDE
PALACES & GARDENS.

The first section of the London Underground opened as early as 1863. Locals called it 'The Sewer'. This poster is dated 1910; it shows us styles of dress in about 1900 as well as the interest in travel for leisure.

Queen Victoria

Queen Victoria (1819–1901) became Queen at the age of 18. The monarchy was not popular; she survived seven assassination attempts. In 1840, she married Albert of Saxe-Coburg; they had nine children. They became popular, living moral, decent lives, unlike earlier monarchs. Albert supported some social reforms and helped to plan the Great Exhibition of 1851.

When Albert died of typhoid fever in 1861, Queen Victoria avoided public life for a while. Disraeli encouraged her to be more active. When she died, she was revered by her people.